ADOPTION

ADOPTION

Margaret Kornitzer

Putnam & Company
LONDON

FOR JOHN ANTHONY
ELLIOTT KORNITZER

Born 5th September, 1956
Died 10th February, 1958

ISBN 0 370 10058 1 Hardback
ISBN 0 370 10059 X Paperback
Printed and bound in Great Britain for
Putnam & Company Limited
9 Bow Street, London, WC2E 7AL
by Cox & Wyman Ltd
London, Fakenham and Reading
Set in Monotype Fournier
First Published 1959
Fifth Edition 1976

CONTENTS

Introduction to First Edition, 7

Introduction to Fifth Edition, 8

1   This Book is for You, 15

2   'Please Help Me', 18

3   Who Should Adopt?, 26

4   'Does it matter if . . .?', 36

5   Where Babies Come From, 41

6   Which Children?, 52

7   Your Child Comes Home, 59

8   'On Probation', 67

9   The Legal Process, 75

10 The Legal Process (Continued), 83

11 After the Order, 87

12 Is it Their Business?, 97

13 Adopting Your Own, 105

14 Telling the Child, 115

15 More about Telling, 124

16 Final Words on Telling, 130

CONTENTS

17 Adopting the Older Child, 136
18 More about the Older Child, and
    Some Others, 146
19 Practical Points, 157
20 Scotland, the Rest of the British
    Isles, and Overseas Adopters, 165
   *Useful Addresses and Further
    Reading*, 174
   Index, 179

INTRODUCTION TO FIRST EDITION

In 1952 a book of mine called *Child Adoption in the Modern World* was published. It was designed mainly to be useful to people with a professional interest in adoption, although intending adopters also read it, I found. Now I have written something especially for adopters, who want the facts but not all the technical information of the earlier book. Although it is simpler in its form, I have taken great trouble with getting the details right, and the typescript has been vetted, very kindly, by a children's officer, Mr. Kenneth Brill, of Devon, and an adoption society worker, Miss D. H. Hillier of the Church of England Children's Society. These two experts must of course not be blamed if any errors have crept in despite their efforts, but I am very grateful to them, and also to Mrs. Geoffrey Edwards who read the proofs and suggested improvements.

You will find here many facts of different kinds about adoption, and these you will have to accept whether you like them or not. You will also find a number of opinions, more or less strongly stated. You can take them or leave them, but perhaps you will treat them with a certain amount of respect because in most cases they reflect views that are held by some of the best of those who, day by day and year by year, arrange adoptions or supervise adoption arrangements. In a way, this book is meant to be a tribute to them.

During the time between writing these two books on adoption I have been doing an investigation which has led me to meet hundreds of adopting families. Of course this is bound to show itself to some extent in the following pages, but the book you hold in your hands is not the book about the result of my researches that I hope to publish, and which I am now writing. This ought to be made plain, otherwise some intending readers

7

may be disappointed. What you will find here is not new in its facts—with the important exception that it is right up to date on law and legislation because it takes account of the new adoption legislation designed to come into effect on 1 April, 1959—but it deals with adoption in rather a different way from anything that has been done before, and above all it tries to be down to earth and practical.

Bromley, October 1958   MARGARET KORNITZER

INTRODUCTION TO FIFTH EDITION

This edition has been extensively revised and some of the material has been entirely rewritten. There has been new legislation since the Fourth Edition appeared in 1973, and the past three years have seen very great changes in the climate of adoption. Many of our old ideas seem quite out of date. Inevitably, the current philosophy about unmarried parenthood, abortion, the 'rights' of children, natural parents, foster-parents, has affected principles and practice. Because of the Pill, easier termination of pregnancy and the still increasing determination of unsupported mothers to keep their babies and not let them be adopted, the number of easily placed small babies has declined dramatically; but there are just as many couples wanting to adopt, and some go desperately around the adoption agencies seeking a child. There is growing awareness of the needs of children who in the past have never been offered for adoption, in the mistaken idea that nobody wants them. But now that the public has been alerted to the fact that there are black and Asian babies awaiting adoption, that there are children with physical or other handicaps who need homes, then the adopters for them begin to come forward. The future of adoption is going to be very much more in the service of these children. People who simply want a small baby out of their own great need for parenthood are already meeting great difficulty in finding a child.

Then we have begun to realise that the adopted person even as a child is somebody who belongs to himself and has an independent identity. The deeper his real acceptance by his adoptive family, the more he can himself accept his differences from them, and accept that he had a different beginning. Even if that beginning was not a happy one it is a part of him and has to be known and taken into account if he is ever to be a complete person. In the past, even professional knowledge and understanding have gone badly astray about the psychological implications when a child is transferred totally to another family. We realise that the complete secrecy and the complete cutting off are denials of something very important. We are still learning, and as more adopted people grow up and become articulate we learn more about what they feel and how we can make amends.

Far-reaching legal changes have taken place. In October 1972 the Departmental Committee which had been considering adoption law since 1969 made its report. The recommendations were the basis for the new Children Act 1975, which I will discuss later in this introduction and in the various chapters. It supplements and changes many parts of the Adoption Act 1958, though much of it may not come into effect until some still unspecified date in the late 1970s. On the whole adoption agencies have improved their work, and adoption agency rules are less rigid than they were. People who have 'own' children, those who have been divorced and re-married and the non-religious or non-sectarian applicants have a better chance of being accepted on equal terms by an agency. Not many people now adopt through a 'third party' and independent adoptions will soon be illegal.

An Act passed in 1968 implements an International Adoption Convention which Britain signed but other signatories have dragged their feet and only parts of the Act are yet in operation. When fully accepted it will provide for adoption orders to be recognised in all the signatory countries. At the moment there is very limited recognition (which does not cover wills) of adoption orders outside the country where they are made.

The Children Act 1975

One important part of the 1975 Act provides for a new procedure under which a natural mother will be able to agree to hand over her parental rights to an adoption agency before the child is placed with adopters. This procedure is called 'freeing a child for adoption' which will enable the arrangements for the adoption to go ahead in the knowledge that parental agreement has already been settled. Natural parents will be able to choose between the existing procedure—when they agree to adoption by a specified couple—or they will be able to consent to the agency making an application to have parental rights and duties transferred to itself in order to free the child for adoption. This also frees the parent from further responsibility.

At present a mother can change her mind at any time before the adoption order is actually made. This can involve in some cases very painful indecision and anguish for her, for she may be interviewed repeatedly by officials who want to make sure she does not want to change her mind. She is liable to have old wounds reopened time after time. Many mothers resent this, and others are deeply upset and their resolution falters.

For adopters receiving a child through an agency, the new law means that once the child comes to them, if he has been freed for adoption, there is no possibility of a 'snatch-back', which has been for all adopting parents in the past a nightmare fear until they have actually obtained an adoption order.

Other sections of the new Act are designed to prevent 'tug-of-love' cases, and deal with the situation that may arise when children are fought over between their natural parents and foster parents who have been looking after them perhaps for some years. When foster parents have cared for a child for three years or more they will be able to have an application for adoption (or custodianship) heard by a court without the consent of the parent(s) or risk that the parent might remove the child before the hearing, as is possible now.

Another part of the new Act is designed to get a sizeable number of children in the care of local authorities and voluntary children's homes into permanent substitute homes. At present, parents who do not want their children themselves, do not visit them, and are unable or unwilling to plan for the children's future, can effectively block any attempts to give the children security with adopters or foster-parents. In future a local authority may formally resolve to assume parental rights and duties over a child after the child has been in its care for at least three years, but only when parents have not been undertaking parental duties or have shown little interest in the child's welfare during that time. This will not affect the many parents who have put their children into local authority care voluntarily, and who *do* care about them, *do* visit them, *do* want them back when circumstances permit.

These new powers were badly needed. Everybody would wish children who are separated from their parents to be reunited with them, and for their family life to be restored to normal if possible, but for many this has been impossible and it is estimated that there are at least 6,000 or 7,000 children who need alternative parents, either adopters or foster-parents. Now, for many of these children, perhaps a new chapter will begin. But this will only happen if the right people come forward to give them a real home, and come promptly. A child-care expert has said, 'Children need what they need when they need it. Providing it "later" is always too late'. Some of the children who are waiting are of school age, and time is already moving on too fast for them.

Perhaps you have bought or borrowed this book to find out more about adopting a baby. But finding a baby to adopt is getting harder each year. You might like at least to consider whether you could tackle the more difficult, but very rewarding, job of adopting an older child or one with special needs, or if not adopting him legally, at least giving him a permanent and legally protected home, as the new Act provides.

You may like to read the booklet, *Children Who Wait*, published by the Association of British Adoption and Fostering Agencies. See the book list at the end.

Private persons will not in future be able to arrange adoptions, and if you want to adopt a non-related child you will have to do it through a recognised and approved agency, either a local authority or a voluntary adoption society. Control is promised to be very tight when this part of the Act comes into force, so you must be very careful—not only when you seek to adopt a child yourself but also if you think of acting as go-between for other people—that you are not breaking the law and incurring possibly heavy penalties.

A natural mother cannot now stipulate the religion her child is to be brought up in, but her wishes will usually be respected. She can, of course, place her child through a religious adoption society.

To adopted people, as well as to many adopters, perhaps the most important thing in the new Act is that, in England and Wales, an adopted person aged eighteen or over will by the end of the year 1976 be entitled to obtain a copy of his original birth certificate. In Scotland this has always been possible at the age of seventeen. Until the new provision comes in, however, the adopted person has no such right. The change is long overdue. There is a general desire for less secrecy in adoption, and a widespread belief that an adopted person has a right like anybody else to know about his origins.

There is a new concept, a new relationship, that has come into being under the new Act, called 'custodianship'. People will in certain circumstances be granted a custodianship order, which is a much less complete transfer of parental rights than adoption, and it does not permanently break the legal ties between parents and child. The custodian has legal custody of the child. A custodianship order may be revoked by a court, but it will give pretty good security to the child short of legal adoption.

The law relating to family adoptions are considerably changed. It will be much harder for parents, step-parents and other relatives to get an adoption order, and the courts may choose to grant custodianship orders instead. There has developed a considerable feeling that family adoptions have helped in many cases to hide and distort real relationships, with unhappy results for the child. It can be a very unhappy situation when a child born out of wedlock is adopted by grandparents or by an aunt and uncle, without anybody disclosing to the child later on what the real position is. It is also felt that many step-parent adoptions of legitimate children after a divorce are unnecessary and unsatisfactory, and these too have been made more difficult, if not impossible.

The new Act is far-reaching, and at the time of going to press few of its provisions have come into force. Some of it is likely to have unsuspected complications and twists when tested in the courts, not least in custodianship where the experts are by no means agreed on all the implications. One thing, however, is certain, and that is the importance throughout all the adoption procedures of the new *welfare principle* laid down in the Act. Any decision relating to the adoption of the child must now take into first consideration the need to safeguard and promote the welfare of the child *throughout his childhood*. This means that the child comes first, and this is as it should be. I have not outlined all that the Act contains, for it is complex and not always easily understood, but in the following pages I have tried to help intending adopters and others to know where they stand—or will stand—under the new legislation and the sections of the Adoption Act 1958 which will continue to be in force. Wherever possible, however, it will be useful and desirable for those interested to consult any available experts on their own particular case—social workers, adoption society staff, court officials, and perhaps lawyers if a case is likely to present real legal difficulties. Adoption is not going to be as simple and straightforward in the future as it has been in the past.

July, 1976   MARGARET KORNITZER

I

This Book is for You

If you are childless and unhappy about it; if you are thinking of adopting a baby but have not yet made up your mind; if you have already begun to make enquiries but have been discouraged by several setbacks; if you have adopted a child and sometimes feel the need for advice; then this book is for you.

I hope it will also be useful to parents thinking of offering children for adoption, and adopted adults too. In addition, it deals with the new principle of 'custodianship', half-way between adoption and fostering.

It is called *Adoption*, but you will find it covers far more ground than the events leading up to legal adoption and the granting of an adoption order, important though these are. Adoption is a legal process, but also it is a very human affair. The adoption order obtained in court marks only the end of the beginning. Happy adoptions develop and grow like every other relationship. That is why a book about adopting a child should not stop dead outside the door of the court but ought to accompany the new family along the road for a while as it sets out on its great adventure.

I am addressing the following chapters in the first place to adopting mothers, or to those who want to become adopting mothers, because that seems the most natural thing to do. Adopting fathers are just as important in the success of an adoption. But in a great many cases it is the woman who takes the initiative in adopting a child.

In theory, adoption should be the result of a decision calmly arrived at. In practice it often does not happen that way, and a couple go through a great deal emotionally before they reach the point when they feel that adoption is the right thing for them. To help towards a wise decision—which sometimes must mean a decision *not* to adopt—is part of my aim in these pages.

Adoption is a Natural Thing

There is nothing odd or peculiar about taking somebody else's child into your home and bringing it up as your own. People have been doing it for thousands of years, and even animals often make good foster parents, sometimes 'adopting' the strangest babies.

The first adoption on record is that of Moses, who was rescued as a foundling from the River Nile by a princess who brought him up as her son. Later in history the Romans evolved a system of legal adoption, as a means of carrying on the line of patrician families. Nearer our own day, an adoption law designed to provide childless men of property with a legal heir was embodied in the *Code Napoléon* and subsequently became a part of the law of many European countries. It was not until the mid-nineteenth century, however, that adoption was used as a means of helping babies in need of a home, so that it became an instrument of compassion and love. This was in the United States.

In this country there was no legal adoption until 1926, although many private arrangements between the natural and adoptive parents were being made long before that time, with the help of solicitors; these gave a false sense of security to the adopters although the signed and stamped agreements were not worth the paper they were printed on if the parents wanted their child back.

Since 1926 several new adoption laws have been passed which make adoption in Great Britain as good as anywhere in the world—perhaps even better, we like to think, than in most other countries. A legally adopted child is as safe in its new home as any child born into that family, and has the same rights and status, apart from the inheritance of entails and titles.

This book, in so far as it deals with the legal side of adoption, is based on the Adoption Act 1958 and the Children Act 1975, which covers England, Wales and Scotland. It may be that we shall have by the end of 1976 a further Act consolidating these two Acts. There are different laws for Northern Ireland, the Republic of Ireland, the Isle of Man, Jersey and Guernsey, which, together with specific Scottish sections of the 1958 and 1975 Acts, will be dealt with in Chapter 20.

2

'Please Help Me'

Like everyone else who is connected in some way with adoption work, I receive letters from people who want to find a child to adopt but have so far been unsuccessful.

I wish people would get it out of their heads that somewhere there is a large reservoir or store of homeless infants who are needing to be adopted but cannot be because 'They' stop it. Who 'They' are varies! Usually it is the adoption agencies that are blamed.

None of the adoption agencies wants to stop people from adopting children. It would be odd if they did, for they are all either non-profit-making charities or local authority committees and, whatever may happen abroad, there is no evidence of a big 'black-market racket' in babies in this country. Incidentally, it is quite illegal to give or receive payment in connection with the adoption of a child, and fines or even prison sentences are the punishment for breaking the law.

The reason why there is a persistent feeling that children are being held back from adoption by the authorities is that there actually are a great many children in the care of local authorities and voluntary societies, who have no homes or whose parents cannot cope with them. According to the official figures published every year, there were in 1973/4 some 95,867 children in public care in England and Wales alone on whom an average of more than £18 a week each was being spent. Babies, who are the most expensive to keep in institutions, cost more, because the standards of infants' homes are now, quite rightly, so high. One may well ask, 'Then why not let all these children and those in voluntary homes be adopted?'

The answer is that 90 per cent of these children in public and voluntary care have families of their own. They are not orphans, and their parents want them back, if not now, then some time. Half the children are 'short-stay' cases, parked out in a home because mother is in hospital, or the family is homeless, or because of some other trouble.

That still leaves 10 per cent. Most are older children, or groups of brothers and sisters, or children of doubtful heredity, or, perhaps, they have behaviour problems. It is difficult to place such children with adopters, although they need loving homes just as much as the others do.

Another group who might benefit from adoption have parents who don't want them but refuse to let anyone else have them. A great deal of work is now, however, being done through some local authorities to find homes for older children and others who could not be placed in the old days. In many areas, children who need homes are being publicised in the local press by the social services department. Some are for long-term fostering, with financial and other support. Under the new Children Act 1975, it may soon be easier to get children in care released for adoption from parents who have never shown any regard for them. This could interest you, unless you do not want to consider any child other than a small baby. But remember, there is an overwhelming demand to adopt babies and toddlers.

Twenty-three Thousand a Year

About 21,300 children were adopted in 1975 in England and Wales alone (the figure for Scotland was as usual about a tenth of the English figure, almost 2,000). Not much more than a quarter of the total in any one year are adopted by people not related to them. Some are legally adopted by uncles and aunts or even grandparents; many illegitimate children are adopted by their own parent and a spouse who is not their natural father (or mother).

This means that when a couple want to adopt, they must locate one of the comparatively limited number of children who are available annually for adoption by strangers. Perhaps they start out optimistically, thinking they just have to walk into an adoption society's office and state requirements. Then they find it is not quite as easy as all that.

It used to be estimated that there were about ten times as many people wanting to adopt as there were children needing to be adopted. The odds shortened in the 1960s and more children were available for a year or two. But though the adoption figures have continued to be high, by 1976 it was never harder to find a child, especially a baby.

The situation is anything but static, but from the point of view of adopters, it is unlikely to improve in the foreseeable future.

Putting You Off Adoption

I cannot help wondering if my first duty is not to discourage the would-be adopter, if I can. Adopting a child is a splendid and rewarding thing, but it is not for everybody. Are you sure it is for you?

First consider the obvious snags, the things that parenthood always entails. Not the major sacrifices, which in a way are easier to accept, but the smaller business of being ruled in all the affairs of daily life by a helpless dependent creature who for years will need most of one's time. Motherhood certainly means for many wives a good many lonely evenings and fewer little luxuries for both mother and father.

Such limitations are gladly accepted by most parents, you may say, so why raise them here? But the restraints of parenthood, which are easier to take in one's stride when one is young, become progressively harder as one gets older. It is a fact that a great many people decide on adoption only when they are in their thirties, a time when we are already more rigid in our ways and find it more difficult to become used to new things.

Married couples often do not start planning adoption until they have been married for some years and have given up hope of a family of their own. They have fallen into a routine. She may be too house-proud, he may be too used to his own pleasures and comforts. They are in a rut, and they know it. The *idea* of a baby is delightful, and so—if you really like children—is the reality. But a baby imposes a kind of dictatorship on the home.

It is possible to apply one or two simple tests to oneself beforehand and—up to a point, if one is honest—find out.

First, ask yourself how many children, all being equal, you would like to adopt? Do you want just one, or, if you could, would you end up with a family of several? It does not matter if circumstances are in fact going to prevent your taking more than one, for it is the desire that counts. On the whole, I think it is fair to say that the one-child adopter, the woman determined to stick at one, is not the most likely person to take parenthood in a relaxed and comfortable way, or to be a natural child-lover. Sometimes she seems to be adopting an idea rather than a child.

The next question is, 'What age do I want the baby to be?' If you have it fixed firmly in your mind that you want a baby beyond the bottle stage, or one who has got past nappies, this may at least be an indication that instinctively you know that some aspects of babyhood will irritate and bore you. It is a useful exercise to sit down quietly and imagine what you would do at this moment with an irritating and exhausting toddler who is in a rage or starting to whine.

The best adopters are tough, resilient and tender-hearted. They love children—not just a child, their child, but all children, children who are runny-nosed, children who are damp at the other end, children who belong to the neighbours next door.

The following is a great test. What do you think of your neighbours' children? And do they like you? If you and your husband always seem to have children running in and out of the house because they like to come, that is a pretty good indication that adoptive parenthood will come easily to you. Adoption is not for people who like to keep themselves to themselves or who are too house-proud.

Let us suppose you have come out of this self-examination quite well. So now you take a practical test, if you can. Borrow a neighbour's baby for the day, preferably a rather spoilt one, and see how you get on, giving yourself marks not only for punctuality with feeds, etc., for lack of fuss and for knowing what to do about wind, but also for still liking babies by the time evening comes. If you belong to a large family and are an auntie who often obliges, then you can skip this test.

Why Not Foster a Child?

In some cases you may be thinking of adoption when, really, fostering a child might suit you better. I have already touched on fostering. In both cases you give a real home to a little one who needs you, but being a foster mother is less final than adopting. Although with fostering there is no guarantee that a child will stay with you for always, many foster children do, and there are some practical advantages in fostering a child that you might do well to consider. Although in the old days it was usually 'the poor' who fostered, this is no longer the case.

There is always a great demand for good foster parents. Ask your local social services department (social work department in Scotland). Under the new legislation it will be harder for irresponsible parents to take a long-stay child away summarily from a foster home. There is now a National Foster Care Association which looks after the interests of foster parents and is very active. It has branches in most places. Fostering as an alternative to legal adoption was never more worthwhile. (See page 175 for address.)

It is better to foster a child who is placed by a local authority or an organisation like Dr. Barnardo's or the Church of England Children's Society than privately. It is better to be an 'official' foster-mother than an unofficial adopter, who cannot adopt legally and never knows when the mother will turn up again to reclaim her child.

One advantage of fostering a child through the recognised bodies is that you are free of basic financial responsibility, since you receive a weekly payment to cover the child's keep, as well as his clothing allowance and pocket money.

Fostering is a useful arrangement for people whose financial circumstances prevent them from taking the whole responsibility of a child. But it is also useful to those people who feel drawn to help a child in some way handicapped, for whom a good deal of expert supervision may be needed for a long period. Again, fostering is also better for the type of woman who loves little babies, but does not want to cope with older children.

So a final question for you in your self-quiz ought to be, 'Do I like children at all stages, or do I just like babies?' For the adopted baby, like any other, will become all too soon the toddler who cannot be left alone for a moment until he is safely tucked into his cot at night, then the school-child always in some pickle or other, then the adolescent with his own problems. One does not just adopt a baby: one adopts a growing child, one adopts a man or a woman, and one adopts for life.

Babies as Medicine

When you apply to an adoption agency for a child, they will ask you why you want to adopt. A little heart-searching about motives is a good thing, but if you are ordinary decent people who genuinely like children, I suggest that this should not worry you too much.

I mention this because motives are strange things. Why does anybody want to do anything? Few of us can disentangle our 'selfish' from our 'unselfish' motives. One day I met an adopting mother who was worried because she felt that her motives for adopting had been selfish ones. The dreadful fact was that she and her husband had wanted a baby because life without a family had become empty and meaningless for both, and they thought they would be happier if they adopted a child. Then she read an article in which the writer said that people should adopt only out of 'pure' motives, that is to say, entirely for the child's good.

'But I didn't feel in the least altruistic about adopting Christopher,' she told me. 'I just longed for a baby and he is the answer to everything I ever wanted.'

Most of the major decisions of one's life, however, including getting married, have a strong element of selfishness about them. I would go further and say that with most of us altruism is not enough; it needs a strong lacing of self-interest to give it continuity and enduring power. A good parent-and-child relationship is, after all, a matter of mutual profit and strength as well as of sentiment.

But there is one big circumstance in which you should most certainly look into your motives for wanting to adopt a child. I mean, unhappiness. If you are desperately unhappy, either because you have recently suffered the loss of your own baby or because your marriage is in danger of collapse, delay any plans you may have made for adopting a child, and do not imagine that adoption will solve your personal problems at this time. It could be that help from a marriage guidance counsellor would be more use to you *at this stage* than an adoption agency. You want to be able to offer a child the shelter of a secure and happy marriage. Nothing less is good enough for him.

Never adopt when you are in a state of anguish or deep anxiety. You may imagine that adopting a baby will heal the wound of bereavement or mend a breach in your married life, but it has been proved a thousand times that it is not fair to yourself or a child to take him purely as a substitute for one who has recently died, and that adoption does not of itself bring husband and wife together. It may in fact make bad worse.

There was a time, not so long ago, when some doctors—out of the best medical motives, no doubt—used to recommend adopting a baby to their emotionally disturbed women patients, rather in the spirit of prescribing bottles of medicine. As a doctor once put it to me, 'After all, my first duty is to my patient.' If he saw a neurotic childless wife making life a misery for herself and her husband, he thought it his duty to find her a baby.

This adoption cure for neuroses of various kinds is now old-fashioned and out of date, and the medical profession as a whole condemns it.

The fact is that adopting a baby will make you happy only if you have happiness in yourself to give in return. There is therefore only one safe state of mind in which to contemplate adoption; an acceptance of your own life as it is, and a sense of security on the emotional side.

3

Who Should Adopt?

It is less easy to adopt a child today than it used to be. The law has been tightened, and there are more statutory safeguards for the child: more scrutinising of one's claim to be a suitable person to care for a strange infant, a minimum period of probation, and the visiting of one's home by various officials until the adoption order is made.

In certain respects the law lays down who may and may not adopt. For the rest, the adoption societies and local authorities when placing children have their own rules for applicants; they must for the child's sake be very particular. But in any case none of these rules is merely arbitrary.

The Law

Let us deal first of all with what the law requires. One important point that should be realised straight away is that nobody has an absolute *right* to adopt a child. The court may grant an order at its discretion, provided all the necessary consents have been given and if it thinks the adoption is in the child's best interests. On the other hand it has the right and duty of refusing an application, if to do so seems fitting in the circumstances.

But you have a *right* to apply to a court for an adoption order in this country if you or your husband/wife in joint applications are domiciled in the UK, the Channel Islands or the Isle of Man, and if you are over twenty-one years old.

'Domicile' and 'residence' are words that have a precise legal significance. There are two kinds of domicile, of origin and of choice: the former is the domicile of your father, roughly, 'where you belong', the latter is gained by actual residence in a country together with the intention of remaining in that country permanently. Domicile of origin is hard to lose, however long you stay away from your native land, and domicile of choice is hard to gain, however long you stay in the new country.

Under certain conditions, which are dealt with in Chapter 20, British people who work abroad can adopt while on leave in this country, while people not domiciled in Britain, including foreigners, may apply for a 'proposed foreign adoption' order which safeguards the relationship in Britain and enables them to take a child to their own country for full adoption there.

You may adopt alone or jointly with your spouse. In the great majority of cases of children adopted in 1975 by people not related to them, adoption was by a husband and wife jointly. Only a few of all the children adopted in that year by people other than their parents were adopted by a sole adopter, and that included relatives adopting.

Only married people are allowed to adopt jointly. That is to say, two friends or a brother and sister may not do so. A husband or wife may adopt singly, but only with the consent of their 'better half', and the court will want to know why a joint application has not been made. A married person cannot apply on his or her own unless his/her marriage partner cannot be found, is permanently separated, or is incapable of joining in the application because of mental or physical illness. There is no legal bar to divorced people applying to adopt, whether alone or with their new marriage partner. Such people are normally acceptable nowadays to most adoption agencies, other than those with strict religious views, everything else being in order.

People often think that spinsters are not allowed to adopt, but this is incorrect. Spinsters may apply, and sometimes obtain an adoption order, but courts are chary of women adopting alone. Adoption by single men or widowers would only be allowed in exceptional circumstances.

A parent and step-parent may not get an adoption order if the parent has been given custody of the child following a divorce. If you are in such a situation you may be directed back to the divorce court so that the court may consider including the step-parent in the custody arrangements. Other step-parents, and relatives, will find that the court must consider first whether a custodianship order would be more appropriate than adoption in their case. Custodianship is new to British family law. See p. 36 for information about this.

A sole father or mother cannot get an adoption order for a legitimate child unless the other natural parent is dead or cannot be found; or where there is a permanent separation; or the other spouse, because of health, is incapable of making an application for an adoption order.

That is all that the law specifies as a 'must' in connection with the question, 'Who has a right to apply to an adoption court?' The law does not put an upper limit on age, and a woman of ninety might apply if she chose. She would not be granted an order.

Be Your Age

Perhaps the adoption agency rule felt most poignantly by would-be adopters is the one relating to the upper age-limit. Many agencies refuse to consider couples who are over forty years of age, although they may allow husbands another year or two. Few agencies will look at couples where there is a great difference of age between husband and wife. A great deal of common sense is behind these rules about age. Many a woman in her late forties who has adopted a child has said to me frankly, 'You know, you haven't the patience when you get older. You want to be young and tough if you are going to cope with children.' Probably the woman who finds adoption a 'problem' is more often than not over forty.

Now if you first adopt a baby when you are forty-two or

three, you may be perfectly able to deal with a very young child for the first couple of years, but, by the time your toddler is going through the trying stage, you yourself are getting on towards fifty and are at a trying stage yourself. In other words you are raising a family just at a time when nature means you to relax a little. By the time the child is in his teens, you are on your way to sixty, and at this time the *difference* in ages becomes especially important, because you may find it difficult to understand the feelings and outlook of somebody forty years younger than yourself.

Take just one small example, based on an actual case. Suppose your boy likes pop music and you hate it. A small thing, and a younger mother can be tolerant about it. But many an older mother becomes tense and worried, and wonders if he is odd because he is adopted; he in turn becomes resentful, and thus are produced the makings of an adoption 'problem'.

Another point bound up with age is one's expectation of life. Most people, if they sit down to think about it, would agree that nobody should adopt a child without feeling reasonably sure of being able to finish the job—that is, live long enough to leave the child at least in measurable distance of being self-supporting. No man over fifty, however young he feels, has that actuarial assurance. Also he will be on the verge of retiring just when the family is at its most expensive.

These are the reasons why adoption societies and adoption agencies of local authorities have these rules about age. If, therefore, you are well over the ages I have mentioned earlier, your prospect of getting a child from them is not very bright, unless you are willing to take a child for whom, for some reason, it is harder to find adopters, and for whom you seem otherwise well fitted.

Among such children are those who are physically handicapped, or have a difficult family history. That you are somewhat over age will not matter so much, particularly if the prospective adoptive mother has been a trained nurse or a nanny or has had some other useful experience of children. But I will deal with this in a later chapter.

In any case, of course, don't give up too easily. Certainly seek a personal interview with your local adoption agency, and see what the prospects are for you. A great many of the local authorities in Great Britain act as adoption agencies. The booklet *Adopting a Child* (see p. 177) gives a complete list of adoption agencies with basic details about whom they can consider. You may find that a given local authority does not place children for adoption with people outside their own area. They often look for *foster-parents* outside their boundaries, however.

It is unfortunate that couples too often let the years slip by before they begin to think about adoption as a 'cure' for their childlessness. How much better it would be all round if they began to consider it in their early thirties! If you have any friends who are trembling on the brink, urge them not to wait too long.

Religious Belief

In the case of mixed marriage, the married couple may be able to adopt a Roman Catholic baby on the usual understanding about the religious faith of the child.

There are great difficulties for Jewish people who wish to adopt a child of Jewish origin. Until now, the illegitimacy rate among Jews seems to have been lower than among their neighbours and when a girl does become pregnant, the Jewish family tends to rally round and make arrangements to help her, so that in those few cases which do occur the mother often keeps her child.

Adoption agencies help Jewish applicants if they can; but there is no Jewish adoption society in Great Britain and, owing to the scarcity of Jewish children available for adoption, the Jewish authorities would have to face a number of problems should they decide to start one.

According to Orthodox Judaism, adoption is permissible but the child, whilst taking his place in the adoptive family, does not in Jewish law lose his original identity or religious status by the fact of adoption. It is therefore vital for Orthodox Jews to consult the London Beth Din (Jewish Court of Law) regarding religious requirements before they contemplate the step, so that they may be fully cognisant of difficulties that could arise in the future when the child is of marriageable age or, if a boy, at the age of confirmation (*Barmitzvah*). For a child to be entitled to full status and marriage under Orthodox auspices, proof must be available that the natural mother's parents were married according to Orthodox Jewish law, thereby confirming the mother's own status as a Jewess. Mere declaration of Jewish affiliations is insufficient.

Jewish prospective adopters should also be warned of the difficulties they may meet in the future should the infant whom they propose adopting be the result of an adulterous union between two members of the Faith. According to Jewish law, a child is not classed as illegitimate by reason of the mother being a single girl but comes under that category and suffers certain religious disabilities if he or she was born as the result of an illicit relationship between a Jewish married woman and a Jew who was not her husband. Fortunately, such an occurrence appears to be rare.

Adopters need not, however, be anxious that the original name of the adopted child has to be revealed at the time of marriage. This is not so, once registration with the Beth Din has been made and the infant's status confirmed. It is therefore always advisable that the appropriate investigations should take place at the time of the legal adoption, so that trouble does not occur later.

Reform and Liberal Jewish circles follow somewhat different principles and regulations, but as the majority of Jews wish to marry according to Orthodox Jewish law, prospective adopters should always make careful enquiries at the outset of their negotiations concerning a baby, so that they are not caught unawares at an important stage in their child's future.

Atheists and agnostics are still not acceptable to all adoption societies, although the situation generally is far more permissive than it used to be. Local authorities do not require applicants to have a religious tie. Non-denominational societies are less insistent on an applicant being an active member of a definite church, but such a society may want to know that the applicants have a sincere religious belief and that they will arrange for their adopted children to have religious instruction.

The denominational adoption societies, those linked with the social welfare work of a church, are of course especially strict on the religious side, as one would expect. But in some areas a Church of England society will arrange adoptions between people of other denominations too (except the Roman Catholics), if it happens to be the only agency functioning in that area.

The Children Act 1975 requires adoption agencies as far as possible to respect the natural parents' wishes about the religion in which the child is to be brought up, and natural parents who care about the religious aspect will want to have their children adopted through agencies which specialise in their particular faith or creed.

Your Health

Health is important, and you should be in good health when you adopt a child. The court will require a medical certificate to that effect and an adoption agency will certainly need evidence that you are fit and well, and would expect you to tell them at the earliest stage of any previous history of tuberculosis or other serious disease, and whether there is epilepsy or insanity in your family on either side.

You would also have to disclose details of any disease or disability that might prevent you from looking after the child properly, or, in the case of a man, affect your earning powers.

Heart disease, high blood-pressure, arthritis, deafness, recurrent dizzy fits—these are a few examples that come to mind. How much these would lessen your chance of being given a child would depend on how serious the trouble was.

Naturally your own sense of responsibility is involved here, and it would be wrong for you to contemplate adoption unless you knew you were physically fit. Before going any further, your first thought should certainly be to go to your doctor and get his assurance that in his opinion your state of health makes you suitable as prospective parents.

If you have had tuberculosis, but are now completely cured, you need not despair of adopting. Provided you can satisfy the adoption agency and the court of your present state of health, you are definitely not barred. Nor is controlled diabetes a bar. Most adoption agencies now use standard forms for the health of applicants, which will be the same wherever you go.

If You Have Your Own Child

Some voluntary adoption societies object to an 'own' child in the family. This objection is based partly on the fear of jealousy between the adopted and 'own' children later, but even more on what they regard as a probability that in any kind of family difficulty or dispute there will be discrimination against the adopted child. It is felt that an adopted child, taken into a family where there is already a child, runs a special risk of being wanted only as a playmate, and not for himself alone. If he disappoints, and quarrels with the 'own' child, then, it is thought, the adopting family will to some extent reject him.

I have seen for myself so many happy 'mixed' families, where the adopted and 'own' children get on well together and form a real family, that I cannot agree with any hard and fast rule against 'own' children. One point to think about is that it may occasionally be the 'own' child who suffers—or who feels that adoption is unfair to him. The attitude to couples with children has changed much in recent years, and many agencies feel that older children and those with particular problems especially are best placed with *families*.

People who can have their own children but don't are not encouraged to adopt. Applicants are expected to offer evidence that they have tried and failed.

Most adoption agencies today rigorously require that adoption applicants are tested for infertility, not because they object to 'own' children, but because they feel that couples should for their own sakes be investigated. An astonishingly large proportion of childless couples have been helped through the fertility clinics to have their own children. But if treatment is inconclusive, people can still apply to an agency.

Your Conscience And You

This brings me to an important point. Until now I have been writing much as if all adopters have to go through the usual channels to obtain a child, that is, to an adoption society or local authority.

Some people do not adopt a child that way but arrange matters privately. I have met some good and happy adoptions so arranged, and there are also always a number of very individualistic adopters who, if their life depended on it, would feel that they must go about the business in their own private way and would resent anybody telling them what to do.

But there are now 190 adoption agencies in Great Britain, though they are thin on the ground in some areas, and third party and direct placing figures are at present low, only a few per cent of all adoptions by strangers. Under the Children Act 1975, independent arrangements will be made illegal at some time in the future, perhaps by 1977 or 1978. But this part of the new Act is being delayed until there are more facilities and money to implement it. Meanwhile, be very careful about trying to adopt a child privately—or about helping anybody else to do so. Take expert advice. The private arrangement is inherently more risky. For some reason it may well not receive legal sanction, and the child has then to remain unadopted and insecure.

But suppose, nevertheless, that you wish to take the risk—and this *is* a free country. This is where your conscience should start working overtime. You may plan to get a child with the minimum of fuss, as you think, under the counter or behind the door, and so by-pass the approved agencies. If so, please re-read all the foregoing rules and regulations about adoption applicants, and consider whether you ought not to apply them to yourself, not just the legal conditions, which you are bound to obey, but the adoption agency rules also. These have been devised to safeguard the adopters as well as the children, and the insistence on the right age to adopt, the importance of good health, the necessity of thinking beforehand of such things as jealousy and discrimination in a 'mixed' family, all these are made much of because the something like 750,000 adoptions that have taken place since 1926 have taught the experts a great deal about what makes an adoption happy or unhappy.

So even if you have a chance to adopt privately, do use these rules as your own rough guide, because you have not been this way before, and because you want your adoption to be successful and bring you joy.

Finally and always, when considering adoption, ask yourself this searching question: 'If I were a child who could choose, would I like to be adopted by me?'

4

'Does it matter if . . .?'

People sometimes ask, 'Does it matter if I am divorced? Does it matter if we are poor?' and so on. This chapter attempts to answer a few of those questions. Let us take divorce first.

Some adoption societies have a link with denominational religion, and their attitude towards divorced people who have remarried and want to adopt a child has therefore been much as you would expect: they have not accepted such applications.

Yet many thousands of divorced people remarry each year. Most of us know couples who have made happy, lasting second marriages after an initial failure that ended in the divorce court.

However, the legal situation in relation to adoption of your *own* child after divorce has changed since the passing of the Children Act 1975. Under s. 10 of that Act, which is expected to come into force in 1976/7, a parent and step-parent will not *normally* be able to get a joint adoption order if the parent has been given custody of the child following divorce from the other parent of the child. The divorce court can, however, make a custody order vesting legal custody jointly in the parent and step-parent; or the court that refused to give an adoption order can grant the step-parent a custodianship order, which means that the spouses then have legal custody jointly. (Natural parents cannot be granted a custodianship order.) But a step-parent cannot qualify to apply for a custodianship order if in proceedings for divorce or nullity of marriage the child was named in an order made under the Matrimonial Causes Act 1973, unless the other parent is dead or cannot be found, or the child turns out not to have been a child, legally speaking, of the original family.

These matters will be discussed again later in this book, but you will see that the situation is quite complicated. Such adoptions or custodianships would seem to need expert advice either from social workers or solicitors or both.

Divorce apart there are many couples, unfortunately, whose life together is poison, not because one or the other is physically unfaithful, but because of nagging, or tempers, or neglect, or because of other habits that affect the marriage even more intimately. For such people to adopt a child is a crime, and I must repeat what I said earlier, that adoption can never bridge the gulf that sometimes opens between husband and wife. Let no woman think that a little (adopted) child will join her together with her husband again; let no man imagine that the care of a child will take his wife's mind off the disaster that threatens their marriage.

There is no happy outlook for an adoption unless the husband and wife are happy together first. Many agencies like a couple to have been married to each other for at least two or three years before applying. Previous cohabitation does not (so far) count!

As well as divorced people, widows and women separated from their husbands certainly will not receive very sympathetic consideration from an agency, and this is so in the case of spinsters, too. The courts back this view wholeheartedly, and although some spinsters are successful in adopting, I have known a court very reluctant to grant an order, even when the child had been in the applicant's care for several years and she was herself suitable.

The truth of the matter is that a woman alone is, from the start, handicapped as a parent. In some countries adoption is not legally permissible except by married couples. But in the U.S.A. there is a distinct trend towards the adoption of difficult-to-place children by spinsters and even bachelors, and this is probably a portent of a similar development here.

Your Relations

One thing adopters sometimes forget is that their relatives have an interest in the child they propose to adopt.

Do they stop to wonder what their own mother and father, their sisters and brothers—even their aunts and uncles—think about the prospect of having an adopted child in the family? Should they ask the advice of any of them? Or are they to spring the whole thing as a surprise? Should they, in fact, care what the relatives think?

Of the adopters I have met, some take the uncompromising view that if they want to adopt a child it is no business of anybody else. It is true there are families and families! Where there is a past history of family rows and coolnesses and the relatives do not hit it off, perhaps there is a good case for not discussing with them what one is going to do. But most families, luckily, are not like that, and many remain close and friendly even after their members are married and scattered to the four winds. It is important to an adopted child that he should be fully accepted as a grandchild and cousin, getting his share of Christmas and birthday presents and otherwise being made to feel that he is truly 'one of the family'.

In these days the greater family, beyond the small group of father, mother and children, is not thought so much of as it used to be, but it still has its emotional significance. An adopted child who is not made to feel that he fully belongs can be very lonely in later life, very lonely and very alone, as more than one has told me.

Besides, the adopted child legally inherits property almost entirely as though he were born the grandson or nephew of his adoptive family; and any property he may have devolves in the same way. He is entirely cut off from those of his own blood. It is, or should be, a case of 'Thy people shall be my people'.

38

The best way to assure a child of a good reception is to take it for granted from the start that the adoptive relatives are going to have a stake in the addition to the family. Adopters should not be discouraged if grandma or grandpa makes discouraging noises, or a sister says they must be mad. In practically every case I have come across, the child makes his own friends as soon as the grandparents see him, or when an aunt, out of curiosity comes to call. The result is a much loved grandchild, nephew or niece.

Your Income Does Not Matter

The things that matter least in adoption are the size of one's house or income, and the kind of work that adopters do.

So far as the adoptive home is concerned, there must be sufficient accommodation to give the child a room of his own, or at least to let him share with a child of his own sex. With regard to income, the only important point is that adopters should be able to keep a child in reasonable security in their own way of life.

I should have said that there is, in fact, one job that adoption agencies may have queries about, that of the publican. I once met a very good publican adopter. When I told him that I was surprised to find that an adoption society had allowed him to adopt, he was at first annoyed, as he thought I was aspersing his trade. However, after a while he confessed that in principle he approved of the societies' embargo on a public house as a suitable home for adopted children. He had been in a different job when first adopting. He thought it most difficult for a man and wife managing licensed premises to give enough time to a growing family, as there was never the opportunity for a family evening altogether. The drink side had little or nothing to do with the matter, for this publican, like many others, rarely or never drank himself, but he did not think licensed premises an ideal atmosphere for growing children, although his own, of course, never went into the bars.

This licensee had put in a nutshell, without any prompting from me, the reason why the adoption expert may not favour adoption by people of his calling.

5

Where Babies Come From

Not long ago, all but one of the members of a big family were killed when a gas explosion wrecked their home. The sole survivor was the baby, and as soon as the news of the tragedy appeared in the papers hundreds of people applied to adopt him.

The same sort of thing happens every time a baby is reported suddenly orphaned. A favourite idea of adopters is that they will adopt an orphan—a baby without strings attached. But parents no longer die young in great numbers as they used to do. The word 'orphanage' has almost been erased from the language. There are hardly any orphans to adopt.

People are also anxious to adopt foundlings whose stories are told in the press. Generous people call or write from all over the country. If it were allowed, every foundling could be adopted dozens of times over.

But foundlings are rarely as alone in the world as you would think when you first read about them. I remember a nice little boy who was left on the steps of a famous children's organisation for which I used to work. The police traced his parents within twelve hours. A parent does not find it easy to 'lose' an unwanted child these days.

Blame Dr. Barnardo

Things were very different in the eighteenth and nineteenth centuries, when thousands of unwanted children were drowned or exposed by callous parents and nobody cared. The lucky ones were those who died; the rest grew up somehow, in the gutter.

You could have had your pick of children to adopt then. It was not until pioneers such as Dr. Barnardo rescued hundreds of children from death or a degraded life that things began to change. If you want to blame somebody for the present lack of children to adopt, begin with Dr. Barnardo.

The majority of children offered for adoption are born out of wedlock. In 1975, out of a total of 21,299 children adopted in England and Wales, some 11,179 were illegitimate. We should consider this for a moment. Although most people perhaps complacently imagine that 'Nobody minds illegitimacy these days', this is simply not true. We still mind, and despite recent changes in the law designed to improve the status of children whose parents were not married to each other, the children concerned also mind, and tend to think of themselves as of little worth, as throwaway children.

Suppressed feelings about illegitimacy do matter to adoptive parents, who, unless they have tried to sort out what they really do feel just may not appreciate that they have within them a repugnance to illegitimacy, or understand that they must face this. Nobody is as broad-minded as he thinks he is, and many many people think that an illegitimate child is somehow inferior and that 'bad blood will tell'. The reaction is as simple as that. You cannot argue yourself out of it. But you can feel your way to a better state.

There is nothing logical about such a natural prejudice. Most of us, given suitable circumstances, could easily be the parent of an illegitimate child. Over 8 per cent of children born in this country today are born out of wedlock, not taking into account all those numerous cases of children who technically are the legitimate offspring of married couples, but where the husband is not the father. Nor does it take into account abortions, or luck.

Today, in theory at least every girl having sexual relations can avoid pregnancy by means of contraception, and abortion for 'social' reasons is far easier than it was. In the present climate of permissiveness many pregnancies start casually and most are unplanned. There is still very great ignorance about contraceptive methods, and popular writing, television, books, make a great play of everybody having a right to 'do their own thing'. In many circles chastity is the dirty word. It is said to be bad to repress one's instincts. The climate of morality has changed, and we must take account of it. In some ways the freer attitude, the possibility of talking about once taboo subjects, is an improvement, in others not; and we must expect another about-turn in public taste and morals at some time in the future.

It is socially easier for a girl to keep her baby under modern conditions, but economically it is still hard. In practical terms an unsupported mother has a very tough time. However, organisations such as One-Parent Families and Gingerbread are pressure groups in favour of mothers keeping their children and demanding public support for it, and these groups tend to look on adoption as an exploitation of mothers' rights. The pressures against adoption are therefore quite strong among unmarried mothers.

But do not think that the mothers of the babies who are released for adoption are the callous ones who do not want their babies. Many of them care a great deal. In many ways adoption gives a better chance to a child of a full and rich life than if he stays with his single natural parent. This is not true in all cases, of course, but on average it has been proved to be statistically a fact.[1]

Here is part of a real letter, the kind of thing thousands of unmarried mothers write to adoption societies: 'If Baby is happy that is the main thing, but I do miss her so; I'm thankful that she was too young to miss me.'

Another mother was still six years later asking the adoption society for news of her child.

[1] See *Growing Up Adopted*, Seglow, Pringle and Wedge. National Foundation for Educational Research in England and Wales, 1972. £2.20.

If you think about these things *before* you come to the point of adopting an actual child, you will be able, like so many adoptive mothers, to have kind thoughts for the child's mother.

Where To Go For A Child

Let us take it that you have read Chapter 3 and have decided that you are the sort of couple who should adopt. Now comes the job of seeking the baby *in the right place*.

From what I have said already you will realise I mean go to an adoption society or the social services department of your local authority, which is really your best opportunity. Do not be put off by all you read and hear about the difficulties of getting a child through 'the recognised channels' though people, it is true, often have to wait a long time, many even when they have been accepted as potential parents. Adopting a child is a long arduous business.

Going on to a waiting list does *not* mean joining the tail end of a queue. It is not a case of 'fair shares' and you are not served in strict rotation. What the adoption agency is trying to do is, first of all, to find the right parents for a given baby. It will try to match that baby to the most suitable people on the waiting list at that time. Because its facilities and choice of new parents are considerable, it usually makes a good job of finding the right baby for you, though nowadays close matching is discredited.

The committee will take into account the type of persons you are, your colouring, your hobbies and interests and also your own preference in children. If you make rigid conditions, such as, 'It must be a girl, of course', or 'She must have blue eyes', or 'All my people were doctors, so we must have the child of a nurse or medical student', you are likely to be looked at more doubtfully than if you made no reservations, but said you would take any child offered to you. Some people want twins. Some would refuse twins. Some would turn down a child with a foreign parent, others cannot bear red hair.

Do not rush impatiently around to all the adoption agencies, putting your name down with half a dozen or more. If you get on a waiting list remember that it takes nine months to make a child, and be grateful if you have to wait no longer than that for some other woman to produce a child for you. On the other hand every agency thinks it reasonable of you to try two or three agencies, although it will ask whose lists you are on.

Many adoption agencies now hold group meetings for those seriously considering adoption. These meetings do not take the place of the personal interview and couples attend them before they have made a formal application. This is useful for everybody. Couples can ask questions without committing themselves, and can sort out their doubts, and the agency can give the sort of basic information everybody wants to know. Group meetings for prospective adopters have become standard practice and, among other things, mean that you will approach the whole subject in a more relaxed way.

But suppose you are turned down by the adoption agencies? For many people this is the big question. In articles written for would-be adopters it is often dodged, but it should be answered.

So many people want to adopt. Because of the demand, so few comparatively are successful. We know how bitterly wounded a couple may be—in their feelings and even in their marriage—to discover that they are apparently infertile, perhaps after years of going to a fertility clinic, which many adoption agencies require. To be turned down for adoption is another blow. Yet if the babies aren't there, they cannot be adopted. The hard fact then is that you have to come to terms anew with your infertility. It is a bitter pill.

You may have been refused simply because of a very long waiting list. In that case you will have been told this when you first applied. But if you have been refused after the usual interviews, etc., this will certainly mean that there is *some* reason why you are not considered suitable. The agency is not able to give those reasons, but they imply no judgment on you as persons. Looked at properly, the agency's decision *may* actually help you. Remember the old proverb: 'Be careful what you set your heart on, for you will assuredly get it'.

So again, the best advice to you at this juncture would be, first, reconsider your own qualifications as adopters in the light of Chapter 3.

I think, too, that it would be helpful if you sought the advice of an old friend who would give you an honest answer; if you have not already done so, also ask the opinion of your doctor and/or a close and honest friend. Both will have a worthwhile point of view. At any rate get an *independent* opinion. Remember, too, that any real evidence that you like children and enjoy their company counts for a lot.

If, after all this soul-searching and consultation, you are still convinced you want to adopt a child, I am quite sure that, whatever anyone says, you will look for one in all the likely and unlikely places. You will enquire discreetly, you will have your ears open for news of a family which is about to have an unwelcome addition to its numbers, and it is quite possible that somebody somewhere will tell you of a baby whose mother cannot keep it. If your mind is full of adoption and especially if you have met with frustration elsewhere, you will find it very tempting to go and get that child and no questions asked.

What is there to stop you? Why should not you do it?

Adopting a baby privately is not against the law at present, although the Children Act 1975 will make it so in two or three years (I write at the beginning of 1976). You must not advertise for a child, however, as this is illegal and subject to a heavy fine. Nor is anybody allowed to advertise a child for adoption. You must also bear in mind that it is illegal to receive or make 'any payment or reward' in connection with the making of adoption arrangements.

If you allow yourself to give somebody a sum of money for introducing you to a suitable baby, you may fancy that no great harm is done. But there is an unpleasant little phrase for such transactions—'trafficking in children', and the adopter who breaks the law to get a child has made a bad start.

Third Parties

Perhaps most casually arranged adoptions have a well-meaning third party in the background who wants only to help everybody to be happy. It may be your next-door neighbour, or the lady cashier in the butcher's, or the maternity nurse where your sister had her last confinement.

These people think they are doing you and the mother a good turn. What they often do not know is that anybody who has anything whatever to do with helping you to get in touch with the baby has a definite legal duty to perform. He or she must notify the local authority of the arrangement fourteen days *before* the baby comes into your care, in order that your home may be visited by a social worker to see if it is suitable for a child. If the local authority does not approve your home, it may prevent the child's coming to you.

You will see from the foregoing that it is not difficult to break the law unwittingly when you start out to adopt a baby the hard way; and it is quite easy to embroil your friends too.

What you will be able to do when the law prohibiting 'third party' adoptions comes in, is *perhaps* to adopt a foster child placed with you privately who has been in your care for at least a year. But the court will look carefully at the way the child was placed with you, and whether this was really intended to be adoption from the start and not just fostering. It seems a loophole. We don't know how the courts will act.

So much for the law. But what practical objections are there against taking a child into your home about whom you know nothing—or nothing but what the parent chooses to tell you, which may amount to the same thing?

The answer to this question is that up to a point there is no reason at all. Quite a number of third party adoptions turn out well.

Also, some of them do not. On the whole, the dice are loaded against you today, because all the babies considered 'adoptable' can be placed with the minimum of difficulty through the adoption agencies, and those who are offered around casually must include a good number that would not be risked by the agencies. There may be a bad mental inheritance; or—and this is a considerable risk—the mother may, despite all her assurances, not really have made up her mind to let her baby go for good. At this time, a mother needs expert help and advice, and, if she gives her baby away without realising the finality of legal adoption, she may panic and demand the baby back—perhaps on the day the adoption order should have been made.

Another snag is that the natural father of an illegitimate baby may, under the Guardianship of Minors Act 1971,[1] ask for custody even if the baby has gone to prospective adopters, unless he has previously agreed to make no claim. This does not happen often, but often enough to make adoption agencies enquire very carefully about the wishes and intentions of natural fathers. Natural fathers of illegitimate children who have legal custody of them must agree to the adoption.

In Chapter 18 you will find information about the 'children who wait', the handicapped children, the children with mentally defective parents and those who are past babyhood, have been in institutions for some time, and others with 'problems'. These children need loving homes more than any.

I would like to see *all* children who suffer under the double disability of being 'deprived' and handicapped, too, placed with good and loving parents. *But that does not necessarily mean you,* if you adopt in ignorance and do not know what you are undertaking. The chances are—I have seen it happen to otherwise kind and pleasant adopters—that if your child is not all that you expect you will think you have made a bad bargain, and, feeling

[1] In Scotland, the Illegitimate Children (Scotland) Act 1930.

let down, you will commit the unforgivable sin of allowing the child to know it. An adoptive father, by no means a monster, said of his teenage adopted daughter who had run somewhat wild, 'I reckon we made a bad bargain, and had better cut our losses.' Very revealing.

Of course, it may be that you or your kind 'third party' friends are willing and able to make all the preliminary enquiries that should be made before a child is transferred from one home to another. You should find out all about the child's health and that of his natural family, the background of intelligence, the real reason why he is being offered for adoption, whether everybody who legally must agree to adoption is in fact prepared to do so, and so on. In fact, all an adoption agency does as routine business should be done by you if you undertake the task yourself. You should also make sure that there is somebody willing to take back the child if for some reason you find after a few weeks that you cannot keep him yourself; and you must also keep track of the parents until the case is in the hands of the court, so that the necessary consents can be obtained without any difficulty.

Unfortunately, with third party adoptions the mother often knows the name and address of the adopters, particularly where there is a direct contact for the purpose of handing over the baby. In adoption agency cases the mothers hardly ever know.

Everything Happened To Them

A married couple I know—good but very individualistic people —collected their adopted family of three quite independently, doing all the preliminary investigation themselves. They did it as well as they could. They saw the mothers in each case. They took children of roughly their own social background; they had them medically examined as soon as they arrived; they obtained an expert opinion, based entirely on the appearance of each baby when placed, on whether the child seemed to be mentally normal. They obtained three attractive children, and not unnaturally they felt rather pleased with themselves over the whole thing.

As a matter of fact, all their adoptions *were* a success—or are so far, with the children's ages now seven, eight and nine—inasmuch as the whole family is very happy together. But for the benefit of anybody anxious to emulate them, I must add that these particular adopters are still young and healthy and very lively, have plenty of common sense and a tremendous amount of determination. They needed these qualities, just as from the beginning, as it turned out, they particularly needed their sense of humour and their sympathy, and the mutual love that could carry them through anything.

For they found that the father of one of the children had been in prison for a series of very unpleasant crimes, that another child had several epileptic relatives in the background about whom they had not been told at the time of placing the child, that the third was the fourth illegitimate child of an easy-going mother, each child by a different father. The first of the children, placed at nine months, had already had unhappy experiences: she used to wake up and scream every night at the same time for six months after placing. Even now she still seems in some odd way insecure. The second child has so far had two epileptic fits, although he is very intelligent. The mother of the third, who lived not far away, happened to be an affectionate parent. She turned up regularly for several years after the adoption, asking to see the little girl and creating an emotional scene on each occasion before they could get rid of her.

Would you be able to stand up to this sort of thing with calmness and courage? When you adopt a child without any of the safeguards provided by the 'regular channels', there is always the chance that you might have to do so. What happens if you are on the nervy side of forty, with a husband who worships success and is contemptuous of weakness and failure? Or if the two of you go through the rest of your life thinking that you never bargained for trouble and that somehow the children have let you down?

Put at its rudest and crudest, adopting a child casually *is* asking for trouble. Go ahead if you are sure you can take whatever comes. If you are not sure, leave it alone. Do not forget that many of us need a fair wind for a safe passage.

6

Which Children?

One may adopt any child, provided of course that all the necessary agreements have been obtained, etc., and that the court decides the applicant is a suitable parent for the child. The child need not be British, but must be living in this country at the time of the application. There is no difficulty over the latter requirement, because, to fulfil the necessary conditions, the child must have been living, for at least thirteen weeks before an adoption order can be made, with the applicant.

The person to be adopted must be under the age of eighteen years and never married.

A question that is quite frequently asked is, 'What is the best age for adoption?' Many adopting mothers would answer this for themselves by saying, 'As young as possible.' With various qualifications, I should say so too. Probably the best general advice to give is: 'Take your baby home when he is somewhere between a few weeks and six or seven months.' A number of agencies successfully place babies direct from hospital at nine or ten days old. I am speaking, of course, of infant adoption.

Sometimes the children come straight from their mothers, but in other cases they are placed first in a residential nursery or with foster-mothers. This may be because their own mothers cannot take care of them even for a few weeks, but in some instances it is done so as to give a baby special care and attention before he is fit to be adopted. Remember that a baby may be neglected sometimes by a distracted mother; or he may be hidden away indoors because the family are afraid of what the neighbours will say.

Such babies need skilled and loving care, before they go out, in a month or two, the picture of health in some proud adopter's arms. I often visit a nursery where most of the babies are ultimately adopted. When I was there one day recently Matron pointed to a beautiful boy of four or five months old and said, 'Do you remember Jimmy, our "Belsen baby"? This is Jimmy!'

Because girls are in so much greater demand than boys, there are often in this nursery several little boys between six and eighteen months who are available for adoption but for whom prospective adopters are long in coming. That is a pity because, although I have seen very happy adoptions that started when the little boys were eighteen months old or more, such older ones take longer to settle down, and of course their adoptive mother never has the pleasure and precious memories of seeing a baby develop into a person.

The Preference For Girls

It is odd that so many more people want girls than boys. Odd, because when an 'own' child is about to be born, most parents' secret dreams seem to centre on a son. Perhaps adopting mothers think a little more cold-bloodedly than most that a daughter will be more companionable. Perhaps they remember the old adage that 'A son is a son till he gets him a wife, but a daughter's a daughter all her life.' Perhaps, too, adopting fathers instinctively shy away from a boy when adopting, because a man's desire for a son of his body goes so much deeper than he may realise himself. A very experienced social worker once told me when we were discussing this point that the clue lay in the childless people who did *not* adopt. In her experience of such couples it was usually the husband who could not face the idea of having a child not his own, especially perhaps an adopted son.

There is also the idea, of course, that girls are easier to bring up, an idea often proved wrong, by the way.

All these things count, at least as long as the child is still not a real flesh and blood baby but just a plan. But most of the people who at first demand a girl and are offered a boy, settle very quickly for the child who is there and needs them. I have heard no regrets later. Perhaps I am prejudiced! If I had the chance of adopting and could take either a boy or a girl, I would choose a boy every time.

After babyhood, any child offered for adoption will come with all the shocks and deprivations of broken relationships heavy upon him. He has already experienced suffering. Adopting a small child is not the same thing as absorbing a baby into the bosom of the family in a straightforward way. After the age of seven or eight months a nursery-bred child positively begins to suffer more and more from the lack of a real family of his own, and needs special care in placing with adopters.

Leaving a child in a home or nursery too long is like putting him in a deep-freeze. If he is lucky he will not deteriorate, but equally he will not begin the process of maturing, either mentally or emotionally.

I knew such a little boy quite well. He was placed in an adoptive home when he was about twenty months old. He was an impassive child with a few basic words of vocabulary, and even at that age had lost some spontaneity, and was a little too good. He was pleasant to everyone, perhaps too pleasant, but he was not loving in the endearingly casual way of most little boys of his age. It took about a year to unfreeze him. His new sister of six, who adored him, was a great help. But if he had been left in the residential nursery for another year or so, he might never have been completely defrosted.

Of course, children, like their elders, vary in sensitiveness and in emotional need. It is the over-sensitive who are hurt most obviously by institutional life. A robust and courageous child will instinctively learn to protect himself better. Such a child may show hurt less, although he may suffer more than the sensitive plants. How can we tell about such things?

So if you want to adopt an older child, do not do it because you think everything will be so much easier. Do not do it because *you* are older. In the first place an older child is likely to be a more difficult proposition than a baby; in the second place, the older the child the younger his adopters ought to be—in reason. They will need all their youth and strength.

The other extreme is to adopt a baby as nearly as possible from birth. There are a good many arguments in favour of this. Many adopters have told me how satisfying to their maternal instinct it is to take care of a baby from the earliest weeks of its life.

I met an adopting mother who has a very close relationship with her teenage daughter, the kind of relationship mothers dream of but do not always attain. 'We are great pals,' the mother told me. 'I can honestly say I feel just as if I had borne her, and when I remember she is adopted it is quite a shock. I'm sure it is because I had her at a fortnight old.'

Psychiatrists thinking of the baby's welfare agree with that mother's view. Dr. John Bowlby, who is well known for his views on the importance of mother love in a child's earliest days, has written in his Penguin book, *Child Care and the Growth of Love*, that early adoption is best for babies and best for adopting mothers too.

But he also had to admit that there were arguments against early adoption. For one thing, very early placing means little or no breast-feeding, which many consider a bad thing in itself. Far more important, however, is the fact that the mother has had to make a snap decision immediately after bearing her child, when she is not in a fit emotional state to decide for or against adoption. Modern opinion in child welfare is against her making a final decision too soon. So too is the law. A mother cannot sign her legal agreement to the adoption until six weeks after the birth, so perhaps you are not being wise to take a child much under that age, particularly as the minimum formal probationary period of thirteen weeks starts only when the baby is six weeks old.

About Heredity

The thing that may weigh most with you, however, in considering the adoption of a very young baby, is that the younger the child the less opportunity there is to judge what his mental capacity is likely to be.

In reality this point is less important than it seems, because although mental capacity is important, 'intelligence' tests given before the child is a year old are really of little use in forecasting mental development. Certain gross mental defects or deficiency are detectable long before that, of course. But what many adopters want to know as soon as possible is whether the child is going to be bright or dull. Some do not want to adopt a child whose brains will not take him roughly to the same level in trade or profession that they have reached themselves. The general psychiatric view is that the best rough guide is the intelligence of the baby's parents.

All the more reason for knowing as much as possible about a child's background. Unfortunately, one-half of a baby's heredity, if he is born out of wedlock, probably remains in the shade. Frequently, nobody is sure who or what the father was—name—job—status—state of health. But many social workers to whom I have talked about these fugitive fathers would agree that a girl will follow the rule of 'like to like', so that her nature and character is some guide to the type of man she associates with.

Two or three years ago, on the other hand, a great authority on genetics, lecturing to adoption workers, said that while certain things may be definitely inherited—a finger too few, for instance, or peculiarly shaped feet, and to a lesser extent physical strength or blue eyes—when we come to the inheritance of mental characteristics we are on stickier ground, since mental make-up can be altered by environment, education, training and so on, so that predicting the way a child will turn out by knowing what his parents are like is as hard as picking the winner of the

Derby. It is even more difficult to predict character and temperament than it is to estimate intelligence, as research on identical
twins has shown. As for ordinary twins, no two could be less
alike than Jacob and Esau, as St. Augustine has pointed out.

So there you are. Of course it is equally difficult to guess how
your own child will turn out. One expert said that while adopters
must obviously take a chance since they are adopting a human
being, they do escape some risks, such as malformation, and they
can choose their child's sex. He thought adopters got better
service from the adoption societies than natural parents got from
nature!

But, you may ask, what about inheriting a tendency to 'immor-
ality', since so many children who are adopted are the fruit of an
irregular union? That is a point that many adopters more or less
consciously worry about. I myself, as you have seen in Chapter 5,
think that, as we all inherit 'immoral' tendencies from our
common forbears, the fear is meaningless in this particular con-
text. Of course some people are more highly sexed than others,
and this presumably is part of our physical inheritance. But to be
highly sexed is to be like a motor car with a powerful engine.
Neither good nor bad in itself, it gives us more power for doing
whatever we choose to do. To counter this, all adoption workers
and most experienced adoptive parents believe in the effects of a
good environment even on a difficult disposition or character.

Before I leave the question of age, there is one point I have
not touched on and that concerns the right age, relatively, for an
adopted child who is going to be the brother or sister of an 'own'
child. Ideally, the time to take a new baby is at the time when
you would probably be adding to your family in the natural way.
That is to say, take a new baby when your own child is two or
three years old, and not without allowing the older child to be
'the baby' for a year or two, and so get his share of mothering
and exclusive attention. He will then be ready to welcome the
newcomer and think of him as *his* baby. On the other hand, don't
let there be too long a gap, otherwise there will be too great a

difference in ages for the two to be playmates. Take your tip from the form of a natural family.

It is unsatisfactory for a child to be adopted into a home where he is *older* than the 'own' child (or than a previously adopted one, for that matter). Newcomers ought to be the youngest in the family, otherwise there are friction and jealousies—all of them avoidable. Do not think this is being finicky and over-fussy. It is important.

Taking Two At Once

There is quite a demand for twins, and adopting two related children at once is an excellent idea if you can do it, whether they are twins or not. After all, you are blessed at one go with two children who belong naturally to each other, and this helps to give them greater emotional security from the beginning. When you are adopting somewhat older children, the advantages of taking two from the same family are even more positive. That is true even if they are always quarrelling!

I am certain that families of children—who have lived together as a family—should not be split up, one being taken by one couple and another going to quite different people. Adoption agencies would not make such an arrangement except in exceptional circumstances, and if you are acting on your own behalf, never be a party to an adoption that means the lifelong separation of full brothers and sisters. Say, 'We'll take the lot,' or don't take any.

7

Your Child Comes Home

A correspondent of mine once took me to task for referring in a article to all adopted children as 'he'. She accused me of discriminating against my own sex.

But writers do not always want to say 'he or she' and to use 'it' too often is like dealing with a bundle of dry goods. I shall therefore unrepentantly go on talking of adopted children as if they were all boys, unless of course I happen to discuss an adopted girl. Sex discrimination enthusiasts please note.

Some time before you bring your baby home in triumph, you will want to get down in earnest to the practical business of adoption. There is an anxious period between your acceptance as a potential adopter and the day you receive the letter which begins something like this: 'You will be pleased to hear that at last we are able to tell you about a baby we think will interest you . . .' and you can use that waiting time constructively, not only in preparing layette and cot, but in learning something about babies.

Probably you won't go as far as some adopters did in a case once described to me by a probation officer friend of mine. She was going to place twins with them and asked what they knew about babies.

'Not a thing,' they said. 'What do you suggest?'

'I'll sleep on it and tell you in the morning,' said my old friend, who had her own way of doing things. (This by the way happened years ago, long before modern scientific ideas were applied to adoption placing.)

The result of her sleeping on it was that she advised the

adopters to have the young mother of the twins to stay with them for two or three days, in order to settle the children in and give the new parents some elementary lessons in child care. They did so—and the adoption turned out a success.

This way of learning babycraft is not recommended by adoption agencies, and would hardly appeal to many adopters. Your best course, if you are ignorant about babies, is to seek helpful advice from your local mother-and-baby clinic; expectant mothers go there as a matter of course, and why not expectant adopters? In some areas, Health Departments extend their mothercraft courses to include women planning to adopt a baby, and a few arrange special courses for them.

Take the simple matter of bathing a baby! If you are one of a large family, this will hold no terrors for you, but many women today of thirty upwards have never had any chance of handling a baby. If you are one of them, a lesson in manipulating eight or nine pounds of slippery infant will not come amiss. There is a correct technique for all the details of a baby's routine.

But do not let me put you into a nervous frame of mind by suggesting that baby care bristles with difficulties. Most women, intelligent or not, make a pretty good job of it. But it helps if you know a bit beforehand and buy a good baby book.

At First Sight

Even if you obtain your baby through the recognised channels, the circumstances in which you first see him are likely to vary. (Far more so if you don't!) If he comes to you through an adoption agency you may collect him from the agency's offices or from an infant nursery. In the first case you will be shown just the one baby who is being offered to you—always in a separate room, and never in the presence of the mother, whom you will rarely see at all. If you go to the nursery you may well be shown some of the other babies, as a matter of interest, but you will still be offered only the one child considered right for you.

Very few adopting parents would want to choose, since this is such a hard thing to have to do.

Before you see the baby, you will already have been told some details about him, and therefore may think you know what to expect. But of course nobody can really anticipate what that important first impression will be.

Immediate recognition and love are frequent. Perhaps it will be that way with you. 'I took one look at him, and I knew,' as one mother told me some years later. When that happens, it is very nice.

But quite often adopters experience no strong reaction either way, particularly if there has been a big emotional build-up of anticipation beforehand. Or maybe the child at first sight is not prepossessing. He may be suffering from a milk rash or a bad cold; or he may not like the first sight of you, and begin to cry. Or it may be just one of those awkward days we all experience.

Being a wise woman, and seeing you hesitate, the adoption worker says quietly, 'There's no need to make up your minds in a hurry. Here, take him, and I'll leave you alone with him for a few minutes.'

So there the two of you are—except that you are already three and not two—sitting in a strange room with a strange small human being in your arms smelling slightly of butter. It is a queer moment. Looking down at the little face, you wonder, 'Is *this* the one?'

Your heart seems to tell you nothing. At this juncture your husband is a great help. He takes his stance in front of the fireplace after a quick look at the baby and says, 'Well, it's for you to say. I'm agreeable, if you are.'

Then perhaps the baby smiles or yawns, or his utter helplessness smites you. In the overwhelming majority of cases that does it. You take him—and you are doing absolutely the right thing.

However, if you should, as occasionally happens, feel an immediate strong antipathy to the baby, then do not hesitate to say so. Sometimes people take a child they do not like either because they are afraid they will not get another chance or because they think the child may not. But an agency should not hold rejection on these grounds against you and you need not fear that under present conditions the child will be left on the shelf, for someone else will take and love him. As for pity, while overwhelming pity for a sickly or unattractive child quite often results in a wonderfully happy adoption, just feeling that you ought to be sorry for a child never does, because if you do not take 100 per cent to that child he will soon know it and suffer.

I knew some very kind and loving people who had already happily adopted a son and then took a baby girl. From the beginning, both husband and wife felt a strong physical distaste for this child. Shocked and distressed that this should be so, they persevered, under the influence of a strong but mistaken idea that normal people should love all children. Fortunately, before initiating the legal process of adoption, they at last reluctantly decided that they must not go through with it. The baby girl was returned to the adoption society. The adopters felt virtually like murderers. But the child was immediately placed with another couple who thought she was wonderful and adopted her as soon as they could. My friends later adopted a child who seemed to be meant for them.

So you see that even if all babies are wonderful, which they are, tastes in babies differ. I think, too, that it is not too fanciful to suppose that the children themselves take a hand in choosing their parents. A child who will play up one couple so much that they return him in despair will go to new adopters and be an angel for no reason that anybody can discover. There may be a deep process of fate going on, in spite of the apparently accidental way in which babies and adopters meet.

Of course it is far easier to return a child to an adoption society than to his own mother in a private arrangement. She may already have made her own plans for a new and unencumbered life, and will be much embarrassed if asked to receive back the child. But that is just one of the drawbacks of the privately arranged adoption of the kind that will soon be made illegal.

Clothes

What clothes one is offered with the baby may depend largely on what the natural mother can and does provide. Some babies are sent out into the world with a beautiful hand-made layette and a few cuddly toys. Others go to their new parents with only the few dirty clothes they are wearing, and not even a change of nappies. If a baby is collected from a residential nursery or baby home, he will of course be wearing clean and adequate clothes, but the nursery will be glad to have these back.

The safest course, and probably the thing you will want to do, will be to bring a complete change of clothes—including the big shawl—with you when you collect your new son or daughter. If you are travelling some distance, put in extra nappies too.

Even when the natural mother has provided an outfit, some adopting mothers prefer to change the baby into different clothes at the first possible moment, because it makes them feel that the baby is at once their own. I have even known women hasten to get rid of all the little garments in which the baby arrived, and even the pathetic woolly toy. That is understandable, I suppose, but I must say I prefer to remember the many adopting mothers who think with gratitude of the 'other woman' who gave them her treasure. Sometimes they will put some small items carefully away until the child is old enough to understand and to want to know something about the woman who was his physical parent, but who is not even a name to him. Such adopting mothers are wise as well as kind, for they are safeguarding their own relationship with the child; but more on this point later. (See the chapters on 'telling'.)

The Girl Who is Giving up her Baby

Perhaps you can imagine the feelings of the baby's mother, but you may not meet her.

Some of the adoption agencies encourage a very brief meeting, if both sides agree to it, but they do not insist on this. The idea is that even if a meeting is rather upsetting it helps not only the mother but also the adopters in the long run. If a chance of meeting the mother is offered to you, I think I should accept if you can bear it, despite the emotional strain. Adopting parents who have met the natural mothers of their children often tell me that they are glad they did so, as it helped them to visualise the child's background and so understand him more. Later on you are better placed to help the child to realise himself.

Even if you meet the mother in this way she still does not know who you are or where you live. The adoption agency will not tell her and the law permits her to sign her agreement to the adoption by people unknown to her.

Naturally it is quite a different story if you make private arrangements, particularly if you live in the same locality as the other party, although it may well be the baby's aunt or grandmother whom you will meet, and not the mother. Where there is direct contact, do make a virtue of it, and try to learn as much as you can about some of the smaller facts (as it may seem to you) in the child's background which you do not know already, remembering particularly that in later years he will want to know something about his natural family and that it will help him emotionally if he is told the details matter-of-factly from time to time as occasion arises. Such things as what part of the country the natural family comes from, whether they are good at sports or some particular job, whether there is musical or artistic talent somewhere in the background, whether the mother's relations are tall, blue-eyed, curly-haired—these are important. So are the details about the natural family's health record: allergies, etc. as well as information about the pregnancy, delivery of the child and neonatal (new-born) disorders.

Even if your baby comes from a good nursery or has been in the care of a kind foster-mother, you may find when you get him home that his poor little body is raw under the nappy. Although, of course, neglect may cause this condition, do not conclude that it is so in this case, without other evidence, for a child that has had the tragically uncertain beginning of most of the babies offered for adoption may already have experienced several changes in his short life. Digestive upsets are one of the ways in which a baby tells the world he feels unloved and unwanted, but love and right feeding soon cure a baby's sore bottom.

The First Few Days

The average young baby settles down quickly and without fuss, although the later a child is placed the more set he is likely to be in his habits, good and bad. If he is already following a sensible routine you will be told something of this when he is placed with you, and then it is a matter of following through. Most baby books agree on the essentials, although almost every mother soon finds that her child has idiosyncrasies that do not fit into any textbook.

If a baby has been for some months with his natural mother who greatly loves him, he may well react much more strongly against change than the baby whose adoptive home gives him the first love he has known. One adopting mother, whose boy came to her at five months, said to me, 'So late a parting from a devoted mother shattered that baby for the time being, and made him from the beginning terrified of changes.' Although quite unremembered, the first few weeks and months of life make a profound impression on every human being.

In any case one of your first jobs after baby is placed with you is to take him to your doctor. Go next day if you can. The adoption agency, if you have used one, will certainly tell you to do this, but if you are acting on your own, it is even more imperative to get a medical opinion on the baby immediately. If there is anything about the baby's condition that you do not understand, even if it appears to be trifling, make a point of asking your doctor about it. Even if it is nothing to worry about, which may well be the case, still you have a right—and a duty—to be sure.

Difficult breathing because of an apparent obstruction in nose, throat or chest, a peculiarly shaped head or a very large one, limbs that appear not to be symmetrically disposed, any suspicion about bad sight or hearing—these are some of the things about which particularly you will have to satisfy yourself especially if you are making your own arrangements, although a baby placed through the 'usual channels' may also sometimes have medical abnormalities overlooked.

Your doctor will know if the baby appears to be perfectly healthy and normal. On the other hand, if he has his doubts for any reason he will tell you, so that you can get a paediatrician's advice. Obviously, the sooner you get this medical opinion the better, for on you will lie the final decision to adopt this baby for life.

Most doctors are much interested in adoption cases and go out of their way to be helpful, because they realise that you are especially in need of advice at the outset. In the past few years the medical profession itself has taken a far more positive interest than before in adoption, through the Medical Group of the Association of British Adoption and Fostering Agencies, which has made doctors as a whole better informed about adoption and has devised improved medical forms for the agencies.

8

'On Probation'

In writing a book that tries to help everybody with all the difficulties that *may* happen, one risks making the whole thing sound horribly complicated and worrying.

Yet, adopting a child is a lot of fun. If you do not believe me, then take the word of somebody who has been through the experience twice. This is the letter of a man with two adopted children:

'We both went into parenthood quite deliberately and only after careful thought about the consequences and implications. We have, however, been taken absolutely by surprise in two respects—we are continually awed and amazed at the happiness and fun that the two kids have brought into our lives, and though we anticipated having to make considerable sacrifices of personal pleasures and indulgences while they were young at least, we haven't noticed any.'

This is not a specially picked letter, and I have read dozens like it, so I judge that most adopters are happy and successful parents from the start.

But of course you are already well on the way to finding this out for yourself. You have the baby in your home, and this is the first step forward. Now the legal side of adoption begins to press more heavily on your mind. The first thing to be remembered about this is that three full months of probation, with the child actually in your care the whole of that time, is obligatory before an adoption order can be made. The three months begin not on the day you bring the baby home, but when the social services dept. of your local authority is told you have the baby (provided that the latter is already over six weeks old), and you should therefore hasten to inform the social services department immediately by letter. Its officer will visit you and make a report to the court later.[1]

You will find the address of the social services department (social work department in Scotland) in the telephone book, among your metropolitan district or borough council offices or your local county council offices. In the Greater London area, you write to the director of social services of your London Borough. In Scotland it will be the burgh or town council, or county council.

Being Visited

Contrary perhaps to your expectations, most of the adopting parents I have spoken to approve of being visited by 'the authorities' and realise how necessary it is for babies to be protected from unsuitable adopters. There may be some overlapping of visitors, but sometimes this is difficult to avoid. A voluntary adoption society, for instance, wants to supervise any placement it has made. A social worker from your local authority must also visit you. Often the latter will call again later as a representative of the court when you make application for an adoption order, but sometimes somebody quite different may act on behalf of the court.

[1] This is the law as it remains under the Adoption Act 1958. When s. 9 of the Children Act 1975 comes into effect, it will provide that when the applicants, or one of them, is a parent, step-parent or relative of the child, or the child was placed by an adoption agency or 'in pursuance of an order of the High Court', an adoption order cannot be made unless the child is at least nineteen weeks old and at all times during the preceding thirteen weeks has had his home with the applicants or one of them. In cases when the would-be adopters do not fit into any of the above categories (i.e. in third party adoptions), the child has to be at least twelve months old and have lived with the applicants or one of them during the preceding twelve months. If the child was placed by an agency, the agency does the welfare supervision; in non-agency cases, the local authority supervises.

Even if you find the attentions of several official visitors a bit irksome, you should have nothing to fear from them. They will not hold it against you if beds happen to be unmade or the room not dusted when they come, and their only concern will be to know what sort of people you are.

Only once or twice have I found adopters really cross about these official visits. That was when, in their own opinion, they were supervised too little—or not at all![1]

But visiting—much or little—is the outward sign of something about which you are all along very much aware; the fact that, although with every day that goes by you love the baby more dearly as you see him developing and learning to recognise you as his parents, he still does not belong to you. Indeed, the law recognises only the mother's rights until the adoption order is actually made; she may claim the child back at any time and you can do nothing about it. If, however, the mother has signed her agreement form and you have lodged your application with the court she has to have the court's permission before she can remove the baby.

Every official person who has anything to do with you at this time will rub this in, and you will be on tenterhooks during the whole period. What can I say to reassure you? Not a lot, perhaps, because sometimes mothers do want their babies back. If you have received your baby through an agency, the odds are that his mother's mind will have been more carefully prepared for the total loss of him than in other cases.

But in the very, very great majority of cases, mothers do not ask for their babies to be returned. Under the Children Act 1975 a new procedure will be brought in, probably by 1977 or 1978, to free a child for adoption before placing, if natural parents are willing, but this procedure will not be available at the time when this edition is published. See page 10.

[1] When the Children Act 1975 is fully implemented, statutory and voluntary adoption societies will be responsible for supervising their own placements and for making a report to the court, as you will have seen.

Legal Points

There are some legal points to be remembered during the probationary period. If you have taken the child informally through a third party or direct from the mother, it is quite possible that at the beginning she may have been paying you something to look after him. You may even have been at first a permanent foster-mother. If so, payments should stop as soon as you begin the probationary period, as no money ought to pass once the process of legal adoption is started.

If you move, you must notify the local authority of your change of address fourteen days (except in cases of emergency) before you actually go. This is for all adoptions.

It is better not to move to a different area during the probationary period if you can help it.

Again, the law says that the child must be continuously in your care throughout the probationary period. If, for instance, he has to go to hospital or be put temporarily with relatives in the case of your own illness, the court might take the view that the probationary period must start again from the day when the child is actually living with you once more. You should always tell the local authority or official of the court when this happens, and hope that the court will permit a short parting to be ignored. Short absences from home of an applicant, such as that of a husband on business, need not matter, but should be mentioned.

The Child is Not Yet Yours

Under arrangements made to safeguard the confidentiality of the adoption, so that a child is not traceable in his new name and his new home, the social worker who visits you after you have notified your intention to adopt will give you a form (EC 58B) with which you can register the child with your own doctor. Don't alter the child's name on his old N.H. card, if this has been given to you. The card might somehow find its way back to the natural mother again.

The baby may have been baptized before he came to you, and if so he cannot be baptized again. But both the Church of England and the Roman Catholic Church have arrangements to cover adoption situations, and you should ask your vicar or priest about them. There are confidential central registers in the dioceses and special certificates of baptism are issued. For children already baptized there is a 'Service of Blessing' in both Churches.

I will leave for a further chapter the question of how to set about applying to the court. It is a big subject and there is a lot to say about it.

Meanwhile, remember always that the *true* process of adoption happens during the probationary period, when the new son or daughter is being absorbed into the family. The legal business is meant to safeguard and recognise something that should already be there.

I had almost forgotten two other points: income tax relief and children's allowance during the probationary period. You can obtain income tax relief for a dependent child as for one of your own from the day you take him, provided you are not being paid to look after him. The income tax authorities will, however, want to be quite sure that nobody else is claiming relief for the same child for the same period.

Family allowances are made for the second and subsequent children in a family; you can claim such an allowance for an adopted child if you already have another child. You can also claim during probation by sending in, not the ordinary form, but form Fam. 2, as persons 'maintaining the child', obtainable from any post office or local National Insurance office. The natural mother must *not* be collecting a children's allowance for the child at the same time.

The above, and other practical matters, are also dealt with in Chapter 19.

'Own' Children and the New Arrival

You may be adopting a second child, or perhaps you have a child of your own. I have already suggested that you should, if possible, leave the natural age-gap between the two children, so as not to cheat the first one of his full ration of exclusive mothering. By the age of about two or three, child number one can begin to understand how nice it is to have a brother or sister and can be brought tactfully into the adoption and made to feel that the new arrival belongs to him too. On the other hand to avoid what can be a shattering experience for a small child if a 'baby brother' is reclaimed, until the new baby is finally yours it is best to say that the latter is a visitor. The older child should be told that you hope to adopt the new baby. Tell him the truth according to his understanding.

It is worth going to a great deal of trouble to prepare a child's mind beforehand for the new baby. If he is jealous—and after all, jealousy is one of the commonest emotions—don't be terrified of it, but treat the whole thing calmly and cheerfully and never allow the first child any reason at all to feel left out or less loved because of the adopted baby.

In every normal family, children watch each other like cat and dog to see that the other does not get anything extra—even the children who are really fond of each other. All parents must hold the balance steady as between the demands of their young. It is part of the art of parenthood.

A wise mother I know, who has brought up with conspicuous success a family of strong-minded children, says that jealousy is like measles. If you must have it, it is better to get it over in childhood when, with understanding parents in the background, you can face and overcome it before it has a chance of doing real harm. 'All children are jealous,' she says.

Isn't she right? And is it just children who are jealous? It seems to me that the world is full of adults who have never

learnt how to deal with that destructive passion. The fault is in
their parents, who in their turn probably never learnt from *their*
parents the way to self-control.

At any rate I am quite sure jealousy is *not* the result merely of
having one adopted and one 'own' child in your home, although
injudicious handling of the situation may have a worse effect
when an adopted child is involved.

Sometimes a wife who has been told by her doctor that she is
very unlikely to bear a child, finds herself pregnant shortly after
she has taken a child into her home. Medical opinion inclines to
the belief that in some way tension may prevent conception, so
that when a woman becomes relaxed because she has a baby to
love, and is no longer worrying, then nature takes a hand and
she becomes pregnant.

Sometimes anxiety can cause repeated miscarriages. One
mother told me, 'Undoubtedly I had an over-anxious complex
which was a hindrance to medical treatment and certainly caused
my miscarriage. Doctors said I was likely to go on miscarrying,
and this, coupled with the fact that I had rhesus negative blood,
led me to adoption. Immediately my anxiety to have a family
was happily settled, I became pregnant and it never occurred to
me I would lose the baby. In fact, as the specialist said, I just
forgot all about it.'

Of course it would be silly to adopt *merely* on the off-chance
that this would help you to conceive and bear a baby. So far as
my evidence goes, it is likely to be the woman who is joyfully
interested in the adopted baby for his own sake who finds herself
pregnant.

But remembering that it is unwise to deprive a child, 'own' or
adopted, of the early mothering that is his due, adoption agencies
now make a point of asking adopters to take precautions against
conception for a time after adopting—even if it seems unlikely
that the wife will conceive. Adopters must promise to do this.

It is a curious but lovely thing that an adopting mother's
natural feeling, when later she gives birth to a baby, is so often

one of deep gratitude to the adopted child who somehow made the birth possible. This deepening of love for the adopted one is good for the whole family relationship.

The Child's Christian Name

I wonder if you will change the baby's name as soon as he comes to you? Many adopters do, either because they do not like the name the child started with or for sentimental reasons. Of course it does not matter to a baby what you call him, although you must be very careful about changing the name of an older child who already thinks of himself by the name he was originally given. A very small child says, 'Peter do it', or 'Mary want it', which shows that the name has already become a part of that child. Change of name is dealt with again in Chapter 18.

When he comes to you you will probably have a new name planned for the baby already, and will call him by it straight away. This is quite all right, and when the time comes to legalise the adoption, the name or names you choose can be put on the adoption order and on the adoption certificate which will take the place of the original birth certificate.

I was touched and a little amused once to find that a couple who had changed a baby's name from, let us say, 'James' to 'Richard', had without knowing it given the baby the name of his own natural father whom the mother had loved dearly and who was killed in the war before they could marry. I have some- times wondered since if it was pure coincidence that moved this couple to pick on this particular name.

9

The Legal Process

Invoking the law is always a solemn business and many adopters find the prospect of going to court for the adoption order a little nerve-racking.

However, do not let this be too disturbing. The legal procedure is simple and straightforward, and normally one should have nothing to worry about. The adoption agency will always help you, if you go to one.

A person who wishes to adopt a child must apply to a court for an adoption order. Where a child is placed by an adoption agency, the agency helps with all the preliminaries; in any case, it will be found that the social services department will give good advice, but you will have to visit the local court to obtain the necessary papers and find out exactly what must be done. Either way it is a good thing to know just what the law is and why.

There are three kinds of courts able to grant adoption orders: the High Court, the local county court or the local magistrates' (juvenile) court, 'within the jurisdiction of which the applicant or the infant resides at the date of the application'. Which of them you choose is a matter of convenience and choice.

The High Court is costly and for most people unnecessary. Fewer than 1 per cent of all adoptions go through the High Court, most being heard in the lower courts, where the costs are very low. They are often no more than a pound or so. The county court requires a small fee, the juvenile court does not.

I am speaking now of England and Wales, where it is not often necessary to employ a solicitor, and never in a perfectly straightforward case. In Scotland the position is different because, although the law there is the same, all Scottish adoption cases, in practice, go through the sheriff courts, or occasionally the Court of Session, where legal representation is normal. If you live in Scotland read Chapter 10.

County or Juvenile Court?

But if you live in England or Wales, you have the choice of the appropriate local county or juvenile court.[1] Family adoptions[2] tend perhaps to go to the juvenile courts, and adoption society cases to the county courts, but there is no rule about it. If you live in a country district, for instance, and are personally acquainted with one or two of the justices, you may prefer to take your very confidential personal business elsewhere, and appear before a county court judge, who is on circuit and unlikely to be a friend. On the other hand you may choose the magistrates' court, thinking it will be less formal.

Very well known people may choose to go to the High Court because hearings there are even more aloof and impersonal (a solicitor appears on the adopters' behalf so that they do not need to go to court themselves). But adoption hearings in all types of court are highly confidential and are heard *in camera*: that is, they are held in a cleared courtroom or private retiring room with only those concerned appearing.

The Rules for procedure in all types of courts are similar.

[1] Wherever I mention juvenile courts, remember that when the new court rules are in force, adoption cases previously heard in 'juvenile courts' as such will then be heard by a magistrates' court (domestic proceedings court).

[2] Under a section of the Children Act 1975 which will be coming into force later, it is intended that relatives and step-parents, as well as foster-parents, will usually be awarded a *custodianship* order instead of the adoption order they may wish to apply for. This is a good deal less final and complete than adoption and can be revoked.

Let us suppose you choose to go to the juvenile court, perhaps because it is handy to your home or bus route, perhaps because your neighbours went there to adopt their child. You should take the first steps a month or six weeks after the baby has been in your care. You cannot obtain an adoption order until the probationary period of three months is up, but it will take some time to obtain the various agreements required for the court to make its necessary enquiries and for the other formalities to be completed.

If the baby is less than six weeks old when he comes into your care, the legal minimum probationary period of three months cannot start until the day he attains that age.

The application has to be made on a set form, a copy of which is obtained from the clerk to the justices at the court. He will answer any queries about which you may be doubtful, and will often help you to fill in the particulars. If you wish your identity to be kept confidential—as you will do if you are working with an adoption agency, or have otherwise been able to keep your name and address from the natural parents—you should when applying ask at the same time for a 'serial number' to be assigned to you. You will be identified by this number throughout the case, so that the other side will not know who you are.

The application is quite simple and straightforward. In essence it states that you, the undersigned, want to adopt a certain child; gives your residence and domicile in this country; gives your marital status; gives the age, sex and marital status of the child (just to ensure that you are not trying to adopt a married person, who is not an infant within the meaning of the act); states who are the parents or guardians of the child and gives the name of anybody liable to contribute to the child's maintenance; gives the length of time the child has been in your continuous care; states that the requirement about notifying the social services department of your intention to adopt has been complied with; states that you have not received or given any payment or reward in connection with the adoption, nor agreed to do so, except as now stated; and gives the name by which you propose to call the child if the adoption order is made.

To the form you attach the properly signed and attested form of agreement of everybody required to give it, the child's birth certificate, the child's medical certificate and your own (for both husband and wife in the case of joint adopters). If you want anybody's agreement dispensed with—say, because that person cannot be found or is incapable of legally agreeing—you may request the court to dispense with it on stated grounds.

Mother Need Not Appear

At one time, juvenile courts usually required the natural mother to be present at the hearing, and this made adopters prefer the county courts, where evidence may be given on affidavit, that is, without the appearance of the respondent in court. But under the present Rules, the mother need not appear unless the court particularly wishes it, and then, in confidential cases, she will be seen at a different time from the applicants.

Perhaps you wonder why a court should wish to see a mother who has already given her consent in the presence of a J.P. It does so especially in third-party cases, when it wants to make sure that agreement has been freely given and that the mother knows exactly what she is doing.

In non-confidential cases, although the natural mother and the adopters do not appear before the court together, they may wait together outside. I remember a case where both adoptive and natural mother sat side by side chatting on a bench in the corridor, waiting for their case to come up. They knew each other well, as the adopters had fostered the child almost from birth. The little boy, three or four years of age, played round their feet, running to 'mummy' every now and again to make sure she was still there.

It was the adopting 'mummy' he ran to, for his own mother was a stranger to him. Although she seemed quite unmoved by this, I confess I felt rather sad to see it, although from every practical point of view the adoption seemed to be the best thing that could have happened to the boy.

The Guardian ad litem

But let us get back to the application. When you have made it, the court appoints an officer called a Guardian *ad litem*—the guardian 'in the case'—to investigate all aspects of the proposed adoption, and fixes a day for the hearing.[1] It also sends out notices to all the persons entitled to be informed of the latter.

More often than not, the Guardian *ad litem* is a woman, and I will therefore refer to this officer as such. Usually she is a social worker from the social services department, whom you may have met already.

Under the Children Act 1975, the welfare of the child in all the adoption processes must now be the first consideration. This is an important principle which is now written formally into the law, and will have a great effect on adoption practice and legal decisions. Sometimes you will find that the Guardian *ad litem* does not come from your social services department; in that case she will probably be a probation officer.

The guardian's duties are many and various. These are some of the things about which she must enquire: she must make sure that all the statements in your application are correct, she must verify all documents offered, including medical certificates, and satisfy herself about all relevant matters. She must interview everyone concerned or arrange for some other welfare official to do so—and particularly the mother and the adopters; she must see that all the necessary consents have been obtained, including that of the mother's husband if she has one, even if he

[1] Procedures for investigating and reporting an adoption case for the court will later be different under the Children Act 1975, when the relevant parts of this Act come into force. For applicants, though, the procedure will probably not seem very different from the way it is described here.

is said not to be the father of the child; she must take up the adopters' references; and she must attend the court when required. What she learns will be put in the report she makes to the court. Although the court is not bound by this, the guardian's views naturally influence the decision.

Agreement to Adoption

Ensuring that the necessary agreements have been obtained is a most important part of the Guardian *ad litem*'s duty, for these are the crux of the whole business. The law says that they must be given by each parent or guardian of the child. The parent's agreement is most important of all, and is never easily dispensed with. In fact the court may only dispense if the child has been abandoned, grossly neglected or persistently ill-treated; if the parent cannot be found or is withholding agreement unreasonably; or, in certain cases, if the parent has persistently failed, without due cause, to discharge the obligations of a parent.

A new, stronger ground for dispensing with agreement is when the parent or guardian has seriously ill-treated the child, who is unlikely to be rehabilitated with his own family.

Very often it is a question of obtaining the agreement of the mother of an illegitimate baby. Such a girl is often confused and unhappy when her baby is born, so that adoption seems to her the easy way out at first. To make sure that she does not sign the baby away too soon, the law requires that she must not give legal agreement before the child is six weeks old. There are medical reasons for supposing that by that time she will be in a comparatively normal frame of mind. When she signs, she does so on a special form (the form used for agreements) before a Justice of the Peace, or certain court officials, who have to make sure that she understands that adoption will deprive her of her child for ever.[1]

[1] Under the new Children Act 1975, a 'reporting officer' will later on witness agreements to adoption instead of the persons mentioned above.

She cannot make out this form of agreement as a kind of blank cheque; if the adopters' names or their serial number are not specifically given in it when she signs, her agreement is not valid.[1] She may say what religion she wants the child brought up in, and the agency will try to do what she wishes, 'as far as is practicable'. She can go to an agency of her own religion.

This form will be produced in court as evidence. BUT, if the mother changes her mind between the signing and the time of the court hearing, and notifies the court, she can stop the adoption.

If the mother does withdraw her agreement at the eleventh hour, the court may conceivably hold that she is withholding this unreasonably and still grant the order. But your idea, as adopters, of what is 'unreasonable' may not agree at all with the view of the court.

However, you have one small right. Once the application is lodged and the agreement form has been signed by the mother she cannot suddenly appear at your house and take the child away, but must ask the permission of the court to do so.[2] If you have taken a baby privately and the mother knows where you live, this gives time to persuade the mother to think again.

Also, if you have had a child in your care for five years or more and give notice in writing to your local authority that you intend to apply to adopt him, *nobody* can then take him away except by leave of the court. You must apply within three months. This provision, which came into effect in November 1976, is important to foster parents who want to adopt. It should help in 'tug-of-love' situations.

[1] Later on, however, when the appropriate part of the Children Act 1975 comes into force, she will be able to release her child to an *agency* for subsequent placing, and in those cases where she does this the adopters will no longer be anxious about any possible change of mind.

[2] Nor can an adoption society or local authority take away a child placed by it, once the application has been lodged, without the court's permission.

It is very important that agreements should all be in order—either given or properly dispensed with by the court at the hearing—otherwise the mother can apply later to have the order quashed.

One mother who successfully appealed pleaded that she had not signed an agreement form and had not been informed of the court hearing, and therefore had no chance to oppose the application. She claimed that for a long time she had not been aware that the order had been granted.

In this particular case the parents of the child were a divorced couple. The father had custody of the child and had given agreement to the adoption. But here is a hidden snag. Even if a divorced parent loses custody of a child of the marriage, his or her agreement is still required to the adoption of that child.

Natural fathers who have legal custody of the child under the Guardianship of Minors Act 1971 have now the same status as parents and guardians as regards agreeing to adoption. Although other natural fathers cannot give or withhold their agreement, they must be told of the application, for they have the right under this Act to apply for custody of the child, and so can intervene in an adoption application.

10

The Legal Process (Continued)

There may be other complications. In adopting through an adoption agency they are unlikely to crop up, because agencies are careful about such things, so that in writing about them I am primarily warning those adopters who choose to 'go it alone', although in any case I think you will want to know the hidden snags.

For instance there may be difficulties about the agreement of a married woman to the adoption of a child who is not her husband's. The court will require the agreement of the husband. When the time comes, the Guardian *ad litem* will enquire into these things, and if the husband is elusive or obstructive he may hold up the proceedings for a long time.

I came across a case where the mother flatly refused to allow her husband to be told about the baby at all. She wanted the whole affair to be kept from him so that her marriage should not be disturbed. At the same time, the court refused to make an order unless the husband's agreement was obtained.

The result was a stalemate. Although adopters could not get the order, the baby stayed with them, but they were unable to provide him with the security of legal adoption.

In Court

The actual court hearing is held privately (*in camera*). In a juvenile court it is held before a bench of three magistrates, as a rule, one being a woman. There is less formality than in open court, although the dignity of the proceedings is upheld. The justices sit with the necessary reporting and supervising officers and their clerk in attendance.

You, the adopters, are given a seat before the table, the child in your lap if he is a baby. When the child is older, he will not be brought into court at once, but the court will probably want to see him at some point in the proceedings.

The whole business has probably been so much on your mind for weeks, and you are so keyed up, that the actual proceedings may be an anticlimax, lasting a minute or two, but the court has already had an opportunity to study the documents and the Guardian *ad litem*'s report. This does not give much time for individual attention.

Some courts do realise the tremendous emotional importance of the event to the adopters, and when they can, they make a small ceremony of it. They advise the adopters to tell the child he is adopted just as soon as he is old enough to understand a little, and they remind them that they should make a new will. (An adopted child is on virtually the same legal footing in matters of inheritance as a child born of his adopters' marriage, but not quite. To make a new will, therefore, is sound common sense.) Under Schedule 1 of the Children Act 1975, 'it is hereby declared that this paragraph prevents an adopted child from being illegitimate.'

County Courts and the High Court

All the courts empowered to hear adoption applications administer the same law, of course, but in the county courts and the High Court there are certain differences in procedure from that followed in the juvenile courts. From your point of view as adopters, the differences are purely technical, but whereas in the juvenile court, soon the magistrates' court (domestic proceedings court), you will be dealing with the magistrates and their clerk, in the county court your application will be heard by a county court judge and, instead of the clerk to the justices, or a member of his staff, you will, when lodging your application, see the registrar, or one of his assistants.

In the High Court, the case is heard by a judge in chambers. The Guardian *ad litem* is the Official Solicitor, who technically is not an official of the court but acts at the request of the applicants. They pay his fee through their own solicitor, the employment of whom is obligatory in the High Court.

Despite all the foregoing, you really have no great reason to worry about the outcome of your adoption application. Although the adoption court is not just a kind of legal rubber stamp and is not bound to grant an order, in normal cases the application goes through without delay.[1]

But what if it is turned down? Then, if you obtained the child through an adoption society or local authority, you must in the former case return him within seven days,[2] or, in the case of a child originally placed with the applicants as a foster child, if the authority desires it. You are not compelled to hand over the child to the mother *forthwith*, as has in the past been done on occasion (mistakenly) when a mother has withdrawn her agreement. Ask for legal advice about an immediate appeal and do not return the child unless and until you are legally obliged to do so. Legal aid may be applied for if necessary. If the child was not placed through an adoption society or local authority, there is no legal reason why you should not continue to keep him in your home, if the natural parents allow it and you wish to do so. But of course the child will not be securely yours, and no written agreement you may make with the mother (or parents when the

[1] Excluding nowadays some kinds of cases, e.g. family adoptions. Step-parent adoptions are being more carefully considered by the courts, and it is not taken for granted that these are in the best interests of the child. See the index. In future, many applications may be turned willy-nilly into custody applications by the court. We do not know how courts will use these new powers when they come into force.

[2] When s. 31 of the Children Act 1975 is in force, the court will have power to extend the seven days to six weeks.

child is legitimate) could prevent his possible subsequent removal from your care.

Interim Orders

Occasionally, when in doubt about the suitability of an adoption, the court does not make a full order straight away, but issues an interim order, which is granted on the same grounds and needs the same agreements as an ordinary adoption order. An interim order, however, has neither the effect nor the legal consequences of the full order. It gives legal custody of the child to the applicants for a maximum of two years.

When an interim order has at least two months still to run, the applicants must renew their application. All those who had to give their agreement originally still have a legal right to refuse, but in practice the same formal agreements usually stand and the Guardian *ad litem*'s enquiries and reports are generally taken as being acceptable unless the contrary is shown.

Applicants are liable to pay the costs of an interim order or of an application that fails, just as they are liable for the costs of a successful application. But as I have said, costs are very small as a rule, unless a solicitor is employed.

After the Order

An adoption order is only the beginning, not the end, for now you really are starting the family life together. Nobody can take your child away. Adoption in this country is unusual in being irrevocable. In many, perhaps most places, including the various Commonwealth countries, adoptions may be terminated for one reason or another.

That sort of thing cannot happen here, and an adoption order may only be upset if the making of it is proved to have been illegal in the first place.

A British adoption is therefore for better, for worse, like marriage; and in adoption there is no divorce, though children may be re-adopted by other people if the original adopters agree.

Many adoption agencies arrange group meetings for their adoptive parents, usually of half a dozen to a dozen couples. Many adopters have already found such meetings very valuable. To say the least, it is reassuring to find that your problems are not unique but are common to most adopting families! If your agency arranges them I think you would find the experience helpful and stimulating. A number of agencies require attendance at group meetings as a preliminary to taking up an application anyway.

The Security Curtain in Adoption

When the Bill that later became the Adoption Act 1949, was being debated in Parliament, a woman M.P. expressed what many people felt then should happen.

'The most important thing with regard to adoption is that the book should be closed and the curtain come down absolutely'.

But there are few absolute things in life, and the 'security curtain' in adoption is not one of them. We may feel emotionally that it would be a good thing to start completely anew with the adoption order, but the fact is that the curtain never comes completely down, and we are learning that it is not psychologically desirable to have an absolute cut-off.

One big reason, of course, is that sooner or later, and preferably sooner, adopters must tell the adopted child that he was not born to them.[1]

There are a great many adopting mothers who, once they have adopted, push the fact of the adoption right to the deepest corner of their mind because they cannot bear to be reminded that they could not bear a child. Never let yourself do this. Never play a secret game of pretend. Accept the fact. Do not try to ignore it.

Adoption can be completely satisfying and happy in its own right. But a make-believe attitude towards adoption must sooner or later cause mischief by making it more difficult when the time comes to tell the adopted sons and daughters about themselves.

There is a moral in a letter an adoption society recently received from a married girl it had placed twenty-six years before. She had previously been to the society to try to find out where her mother was. The adopters had given her her adoption order, but this contained only the temporary address of the mother. At the adoption society she was advised not to pursue her quest

[1] Indeed, by the end of 1976 we shall be experiencing the effects of the Children Act 1975, when s. 26 comes into force, giving adopted people over the age of eighteen the right to information about their birth records. (The age is still seventeen in Scotland.) This has come about because of the new feeling about honesty and openness in adoption matters. Adopted people already feel that they have a moral right to know details of their birth. This is admittedly hard on natural parents who have felt securely anonymous. But despite what many think, there has never been any legal guarantee of secrecy, though that has been the *effect* of the law until now. See Chapters 14 to 16.

any further, for fear of upsetting any new life the mother had been able to make for herself, and the adopted girl was able to accept this advice because she had had a happy home life with adoptive parents who had not tried to keep the facts from her.

She wrote: 'It has been such a joy to meet you after all these years and I would like to thank you for your great kindness to me, not only when I visited you the other day, but twenty-six years ago, when you made it possible for me to have a new start. If I am your only "baby" to find such happiness, then your life's work is amply rewarded.

'With regard to my mother, I do not wish anyone any heart-break, but if at any time it is possible, do tell her that she did the right thing and that I have often thought of her and hope she has found a measure of the happiness which I have had and am having now. If she wishes to contact me, I shall be overjoyed. I have been very happy and you can see that life has treated me well. My adopting mother is a very brave and wonderful person.

'To speak to someone who has actually come face to face with my mother is something beautiful which I shall never forget.'

This letter is evidence of ties of love and affection which bind adopted girl, natural mother and adoptive mother together in a relationship which has joy in it; and this was able to grow because the adoptive parents were wise enough to provide the right atmosphere, an atmosphere compounded of understanding and truth.

The Legal Effects of an Adoption Order

The effect of an adoption order is that the adopted child shall be treated in law, where the adopters are a married couple, as if he had been born as a child of the marriage—even if he was born before they were married!—or in the case of people adopting alone, as if he had been born to the adopter in wedlock, but not as the child of any actual marriage of the adopter.

Among other things this means that adopter and adopted child come within the prohibited degrees of consanguinity, that is, they must not marry one another. But the law says nothing about brothers and sisters in this connection, so there is nothing against adoptive brothers and sisters marrying each other, and Parliament deliberately meant this to be so.

Inheritance

The position in all Great Britain is now that if the adopter, the adoptee or anybody else dies intestate after the adoption order is made, the property devolves exactly as though the adopted child were the natural-born child of the adopters (apart from entails arranged before the date of the adoption order.)

Under the Children Act 1975, an adopted child is deemed to be the legitimate child of his adopters, practically to the exclusion of all former ties. If a single mother now adopts her own child, she has no further right to payments for the child from the natural father, who has no further rights or duties towards the child.

Children adopted on or after 1 January 1976 have virtually the same rights of inheritance as natural children born in wedlock to the adopters, whether or not a will or deed was made before the adoption. But this extension of the adopted person's rights is *not retrospective*. That is to say, it does not apply to a deed already *executed* before 1 January 1976, or to the will of a person dying before that date.

Also, where an adopter makes a will referring to 'my child' or 'my children', but does not mention specific names, this is taken to include any adopted children. The wills of adoptive grandparents, uncles and aunts and other relations are also interpreted in this way.

Because of possible complications which testators may not foresee, however, those with adopted children are always well advised to make a new will, naming the adopted child as a beneficiary, when adopting. It is not always enough to add a codicil to an existing will. A fee for a properly drafted will may well save a great deal of worry and anxiety later on, for in spite of the clear wording of the Act, difficulties do crop up from time to time when wills involving an adopted person go to probate. If in any doubt, consult a solicitor.

Another point that I can merely touch upon here is that the world today in terms of speedy communication is smaller than it was, yet there are just as many national jurisdictions as ever, and as many different adoption laws as there are countries. Since 16 July 1964, under a new Act all adoptions made anywhere in the British Isles, except Eire, have been fully recognised in Great Britain. In 1968 Parliament passed the Adoption Act 1968, which gave effect to the International Adoption Convention ratified by this country in 1964, under which the signatory countries recognise each other's adoptions. The 1968 Act, however, does not cover all adoptions made in all countries outside the U.K., and as it is complex and difficult and cannot be simplified or easily summarised,[1] British subjects adopting a child overseas who need advice on the legal position should consult a lawyer skilled in international law or in adoption law. All sections of the Act are not yet in force. Previous to its passing—and even now to a great extent—adoptions have never been fully recognised in any other country than the ones where the orders were actually made, even as between countries in the Commonwealth. New Zealand alone, as a pioneer, recognises adoptions wherever made. All this means that you should omit no precautions within your power to make sure that your adopted child gets by inheritance all he is intended to receive.

Entails and estates accompanying a title, as well as titles themselves, are excluded from the effects of an adoption order,

---

[1] Indeed so far it has not been ratified by most of the participating countries.

so that inheritance of these things within a family continues to be exactly as though the adoption had never happened.

When an adopted child acquires rights of inheritance in his new family, he at the same moment loses all such rights in his natural family, again excepting only entailed estates and titles.

If you adopt a child who has been legally adopted before, only the latest adoption counts. The effect of previous adoptions is completely effaced, except that nobody may marry a person they have once adopted, even if the adoption has been cancelled out by a subsequent adoption.

Foreign Children and Adopters

You may adopt a foreign child in Britain, and if you are a British subject (or if the husband is, in the case of an adopting couple), the child becomes British too when the adoption order is made. Foreign children adopted in England, Wales or Scotland by citizens of Northern Ireland and the Republic of Ireland also become British.

But if you are an American, or of any other non-British nationality, although you can fully adopt here if you are domiciled as well as resident in this country (see Chapter 3), or obtain a provisional adoption order if not domiciled here (see Chapter 10), a British adoption order does not make the child you adopt British if he was not so already. On the other hand, a British child adopted in this country by aliens remains British. Only the country to which the adopters belong can grant its citizenship to their adopted child, on such terms as it may lay down. Some countries do not allow their nationals to adopt abroad, except by express permission.

The Adoption Order and the New Certificate

Having adopted, you are sent an abridged copy of the *adoption order*, which contains the child's original name. You can ask for a full copy if you want it, and this names the natural parents. An extract from the Adopted Children Register, now in Hampshire[1] (or Edinburgh, in the case of Scotland), popularly called 'the new birth certificate', can be obtained just as you get a birth certificate, which is really a certified copy of an extract from the Register of Births, and adopted people use it just like a birth certificate.

The full certificate contains the following information: date and country of birth (and, in England and Wales since 1959, district and sub-district), name and surname and sex of child, name and surname, address and occupation of adopter or adopters, date of the adoption order and description of the court which made it. You can also get the short certificate, which gives only name, surname, sex, date and place of birth and is practically indistinguishable from an ordinary short birth certificate, as it does not mention adoption, unless the child was born, or adopted, outside England. You will be sent a free copy of the short certificate.

When you get your child a short certificate, you should help forward the main purpose for which it was instituted by taking out similar certificates for all the family. They are cheap and handy and can be used for most purposes, e.g. getting a passport.

But what happens to the original entry in the Register of Births relating to a child subsequently adopted?

The Registrar General is directed to mark this 'adopted', but it remains in the register. It is a record of fact and cannot be obliterated. However, in the case of adoption orders granted in England and Wales there is no way of linking up the person mentioned in the Births entry with the person entered on the Adopted Children Register, without the order of a competent court, except that an adopted person himself now has access to his original birth record.

[1] The address is Titchfield, Fareham, Hants., telephone 032-944 2511, extension 288.

Courts have rarely been asked to grant permission for the original identity of an adopted child to be known. In 1956 a court allowed a child to be traced through the Adopted Children Register because some money had been left to him specifically through the natural family, and the judge thought it was right he should have it. But psychological reasons have not counted for much.

At the end of 1976, however, the situation will be changed when adopted people will have the right to know what is in their birth record. They will have this right on attaining the age of eighteen (seventeen in Scotland), although if they were adopted before the passing of the Children Act 1975, they will have to see personally a 'counsellor' either at the General Register Office in London, or in Edinburgh, or alternatively at a specified social services office or voluntary adoption society. This will be a definite condition.

Insurance, Income Tax, Family Allowances

An adopted child is in the position of a natural child of his adopters in connection with industrial insurances, income tax and family allowances. Also an 'adopted' child—and this is so whether the adoption is legal or only *de facto* (i.e., where the child lives with you permanently and is commonly accepted as your child)—can take on a protected tenancy from an adoptive parent or grandparent if he was living with that person when the latter died.

Do bear in mind that no statutory or other body ought to discriminate against your adopted child as such, or demand any information that is not on the copy of the new adoption certificate. Sometimes local clerks or lower grade officials (even senior officials have been known to err) are ignorant of the adoption law, but one should never accede to any request to see the original order, for instance, or give any information about the child's birth that does not appear on the adoption certificate.

If you think that information is being wrongfully demanded, or that action is being taken which is prejudicial to your child because he is adopted, get in touch with the Association of British Adoption and Fostering Agencies, see address at the end. This organisation has been able to clear up many points satisfactorily with such bodies as the Commissioners for Inland Revenue and the three Services.

Parish Registers and Baptism

Some children are baptized before being placed, for adoption. Sometimes adopters do not know whether the child has been baptized or not. In the first case, the adopters cannot have the child re-baptized. 'People come to me and ask me to do Tommy again, and are quite put out when I say it cannot be done,' a vicar told me. 'They seem to think it is like a vaccination which hasn't taken!'

But to provide for such cases the Church of England Information Board provides forms for a shortened form of baptismal certificate which gives only the child's name and the date of the ceremony. Your vicar will advise you on what to do.

In the Roman Catholic Church, where reference to baptismal certificates is more frequently needed throughout life, everything to do with these certificates is far more highly organised. A special baptismal certificate is issued after the adoption order is made, giving the child's adopted name only, and the original certificate is held by the diocesan authorities.

If it is uncertain whether the child was baptized or not, children can be conditionally baptized in either Church.

In the Church of England, as for Roman Catholics, there is also a 'Service of Blessing' for those who feel they would like to mark the adoption in this way. The C. of E. 'Service of Blessing Upon the Adoption of a Child' (Church House Bookshop, Great Smith Street, London, S.W.1) is not denominational in form and may be of value to adopters who are not members of the Church of England.

95

Looking well ahead to the marriage of an adopted child, nowadays it is regarded as correct procedure for an adoptive father's name to be entered in the register as if he were the natural father.

Research

Under Regulations which came into force in 1965 adoption agencies, both voluntary societies and those set up by local authorities, may permit information obtained about individual cases to be disclosed to researchers approved by the Dept. of Health and Social Security, without the consent of the people involved. If you are concerned about confidentiality, you should ask the agency about its policy in regard to research by outside persons.

Is it Their Business?

So far I have dealt only with the legal and official effects of the adoption order. These are important because they provide a kind of safe scaffolding inside which a happy family life together can be built up. But of course many other results flow from adopting a baby.

These are *feelings*, not *facts*, but they are none the less important for that.

It is important, for instant, to start off with kind feelings for the woman who actually bore the child. I have always remembered what an adopting mother told me once. She said, 'Whenever Sue has a birthday I think of her mother on that day.' It is a good and fruitful thing to think of the mother, and pray for her. Many natural mothers never forget the babies they have borne, and even though they think that by letting them be adopted they have done their best for them, they still sometimes wonder. Another adopting mother told me, 'When I think of the boy's mother, I am terribly grateful to her. She gave me the most wonderful present I ever had.'

Remembering that other woman at times such as Christmas and birthdays, when your thoughts and wishes for the child must be joined together for his happiness is, I am sure, a wonderful thing for keeping the relationship with your child secure and sweet.

But on the practical plane, what is to be done about further contact with the natural family once the adoption is made?

This problem does not arise when the adoption has been arranged through the recognised channels, since the mother does not know who or where the adopters are. The only small point that may arise is whether you should agree to let the mother have a photograph of the baby. The mother may well ask for this, and certainly it is a thing you can safely do and in fact you should do it. If the mother makes other requests, the society will deal with them.

But when you have made your own arrangements, or your whereabouts are known to the mother, there is always a fair chance that after the order is made she will be loth to break the connection entirely—whatever promise she may have made beforehand—and will ask if she can see the baby sometimes.

Such a request is hard to refuse, but I think you must say no. However good a person the mother may be, it can do the child nothing but harm to be brought up knowing two mothers or perhaps suspecting that an emotional 'auntie' who visits sometimes is really somebody closer to him. Even if the mother says she only wants to see the baby once or twice, it is always difficult to know when or where to draw the line.

It is easier and better all round, in the long run, to end all contact at once. Some of the wisest adopters I have known were a couple who had actually been personal friends of the natural mother. She and the adopting mother had been at school together. But after the adoption, both sides agreed that it would be better if there were no further contact whatever, even by letter. One side moved right away and the connection was completely broken off. They were, I think, doing the right thing from the point of view of the child and of everybody else—certainly until the child grew up.

If the mother persists in writing, or even calls, when asked not to do so, then perhaps a solicitor's letter will be necessary. This is usually enough warning even in tough cases, but if the mother still persists, the right not to be molested by her can be upheld in law.

Breaking off relations goes for natural 'grannies' and other relatives too, as a rule, though it is very hard luck on a grandparent who loves her daughter's baby and opposed his adoption to lose him for ever to strangers. But there can be exceptions here. I would say that sometimes it is a good thing for a natural grand-parent or aunt to keep up some contact, but only in a case where there has not been much secrecy in any case and where both sides are easy-going and kindly disposed to each other. Everything here depends on circumstances. But remember it is the adopters' right to choose.

Further Contact With The Society

It is for adopters to choose too whether they want future visits from representatives of adoption societies or local authorities who have helped in the adoption. Legally the agencies have no right under the Adoption Act to maintain the connection and, if you do not want such visits say so. On the other hand, an occasional tactful and friendly caller may be useful in the early days. In any case, like many other people, you may feel you want to maintain some contact for a while with the adoption agency.

About donations, if you have used a *voluntary* society: although there is a common idea that adoption societies are official bodies paid for out of the rates, or otherwise well subsidised, they badly need your help. Adoption societies are registered charities which cannot legally charge fees for their services. The cost of arranging an adoption, in time, overheads and incidental expenses, may be £100 or £150 or even more. Yet delighted and grateful adopters often think they have settled their moral debt to an adoption society by giving a pound or five pounds. Some adoption societies now ask adopters to pay an agreed sum towards expenses; this is *not* a fee, which is forbidden by law. Local authorities do not ask for expenses or donations, to my knowledge, though there is no bar to their doing so.

Your Relations, Friends and Neighbours

Finally, what should one's own relatives, friends and neighbours be told about the adoption? What information, if any, is to be given to the child's school, when the time comes?

I have met adopters who say, 'We did not let any of our relations know when we were adopting Alec (or Alison). Why should we? It was none of their business.'

On that score, we all know that there are some awkward families. Some people never agree with their parents and brothers and sisters and once they have left home do not meet them from one year's end to the other. Where contact continues, there may be constant friction and jealousy over big things and small.

But people usually agree reasonably well with their relatives and in-laws, and even today, when the wider family seems to matter so much less than it did, relations do count, as I have mentioned in Chapter 4, and friendship with them can be one of the pleasures of life.

To say that the adoption of a child is nobody's business but that of the adoptive parents appears to me to be pure nonsense. The adoption is important to those who have just become adopting grandparents, and it matters to adoptive uncles and aunts and cousins. The child belongs in the family, and should feel from the beginning that he does, and the family should feel that he belongs and should have every chance to welcome him. If, as he grows up, he feels that he is being left out in the cold, he will feel first bewildered and then lonely and, perhaps, bitter. He has, after all, been deprived by law of all his blood relations, and has a right to be properly introduced to his adoptive ones. In fact one of the important elements of the security that you hope to give your adopted child is the family background and family recognition with which you endow him.

Behind the attitude of the adopters who say, 'It is not my parents' business if I adopt a child', there is one motive, fear.

They are afraid of criticism, even hostility, and they are prepared to defend their actions before the battle commences.

But in the ordinary way such fears are groundless. I will not pretend that one's nearest and dearest will not exercise the right to criticise the intention to adopt. Criticism is a family privilege. But it is always worth discussing one's intentions with one's own people and hearing their views. Adopters have found that those who say, 'I could never feel the same about an adopted child as about a grandchild of my own,' are the ones who usually go down like nine-pins when the flesh-and-blood child is placed for the first time in their arms. A baby is a great ambassador for his own rights.

I met Peter when he was a boy of eight, a confident child with a chuckle, and a twinkle in his eye. He was not like the wistful baby Peter who stared at me out of the pages of the family album of snapshots.

'My mother is one of the old school,' said Peter's adopting mother. 'When I wrote and told her we were adopting him she answered that she did not approve at all. She said that I was laying up trouble for myself, that I did not know how he would turn out and that for her own part, while she would be kind and just to the child—I always remember her words—we must not expect her to love him.'

Peter's mother laughed. 'She descended on us the day after he arrived, told me roundly that I knew nothing about looking after babies—which was true—picked him up and said, "Poor little thing. It's obvious he needs us," and became quite the most doting grandmother I've ever seen. Father was just as bad. My brother's children were growing up, so they were thrilled to have a baby in the family again.'

I am always coming across cases where the adopted child is the favourite grandchild—according to the proud adopters. If that were literally true, it would be hard on the 'own' children, but I do know it is just because adopters behave and think as people do with children born to them—their child is marvellous.

In many cases, adopting aunts and uncles seem to take the advent of the child for granted, especially nowadays when adoption is such a common occurrence. Nevertheless you should never neglect to cultivate good family feelings in all the usual ways, by taking every chance of showing off the new baby, by visits and invitations and by sending news and photographs.

On the lowest plane—but this really does matter a great deal to a child—you want your new son or daughter to receive his quota of birthday and Christmas presents and cards. Also, he has inheritance rights in the extended family in the same way as any other son or daughter of yours.

Do Not Discuss Origins

Telling your relations all about the child's original background is another thing. Those adopters who tell little or nothing to anybody are the wise ones. *This* really is nobody else's business. The documents should be kept in a safe place, best of all in a safe deposit, otherwise in a properly locked drawer to which there is no casual access. To curious questions the right answer is, 'We have forgotten all that. He is our boy now and the past is a closed book.' That goes, of course, not only for relations but also for friends and the neighbours.

Again, should friends be told that a child has been adopted? This is a case, I think, where the adoption is not any of their business; but a great deal depends on circumstances. You may live in a place where everybody knows about the adoption, and cannot help knowing, right from the beginning. In such a case the only thing to do is to be frank and easy and natural about it, but not make too much of it. Or you may live in a town flat where you could pass off the child as your own, without anybody knowing any better. What you tell your neighbours then is for you to decide. Perhaps the best rule in that case is not to volunteer the information, but on the other hand never conceal the fact with a lie.

One of my favourite adoption stories is about two young brothers: one was asked which of them was adopted. He answered, 'One of us is, but I can't remember whether it's him or me.'

Some people's frankness, well meant though it may be, can be badly overdone. I think of the kind of adoptive mother who introduces her child to a chance acquaintance with the rather aggressive words, 'He's adopted, you know.' Small children will not mind this, may even be rather proud of it, in fact. But older children usually squirm inwardly at being introduced as something a bit different from other children. They hate it, and one can never be quite sure at what stage, or why, a child's attitude to such an introduction will change from pride to embarrassment. We grossly underrate the understanding of children and their ability to take in what is said about them in their hearing. Little pitchers do have long ears. A classic lesser-horror story—quite true—is the one about the mother who took her small son, aged five, to the psychiatrist and while the child was in the same room said, 'Of course he has no idea he is adopted!'

One of the troubles that may arise out of telling the details of your adopted child's past history to your best friend is that, without meaning any harm, she may relate them to her husband in the hearing of her own children. This can easily happen.

Should The School Be Told?

Some people tell their child's school about his adoption, some do not. Here again a good deal depends on circumstances. There is a good deal to be said for keeping to the rule of telling nobody until you need, although examinations and scholarships may force the issue if the production of a birth certificate is required.

Where a sympathetic headmaster or headmistress is put into a stronger position to help an adopted child through his difficulties by knowing all the circumstances, then there must be a good case for telling. That is perhaps particularly important if you live in an unsympathetic neighbourhood and a risk of bullying or gossip by other children exists.

But, summing up, I would say that as a rule least said is soonest mended. Some of the happiest adoptions are helped when parents tell their adopted son or daughter, 'This is our secret. *We* can talk about it together if we like. But we won't discuss it with anybody else.' I am quite sure this is the attitude most adopted children prefer. If at some later stage they themselves voluntarily decide to tell one or more of their own friends, as they probably will, then that is very much their business and quite a different thing.

The golden rule always is not to make adoption a furtive secret or a shameful one, for *whatever reason*. Adoption can never be a thing dead and buried for ever—there will be more about this in a later chapter—but on the other hand it is neither dreadful nor unusual.

The ideal situation is where everybody knows about the adoption and nobody wants to gossip about it; but this depends on the neighbourhood in which you live—some districts, streets, villages, being, according to adopters, very kind places, whereas others, quite near, perhaps, seem to show nothing but malice and meanness towards adopting families. But this in turn may depend upon whether you live in good fellowship with those who are around you, and that again depends on other things, outside the scope of this book.

13

Adopting Your Own

Until now I have been writing mainly about adoptions in which the child is not related to the adopters, but thousands of children are adopted by relatives each year.

Let the statistics speak. Out of about 10,170 adoptions of legitimate children in 1975, some 9,262 children were adopted by couples one or both of them a parent, usually after a divorce. In the case of children born out of wedlock, almost 5,305 out of the total number of about 11,180 illegitimate children adopted during the year were adopted by the mother and her husband. In about 100 cases the parent adopted her/his child as 'sole adopter'.[1]

By far the largest group of family adoptions is therefore composed of adoptions by the parent and the new partner adopting jointly. There are also some adoptions by uncles and aunts, or perhaps in some cases grandparents. 'Relative' has a special meaning under the Act, and signifies 'a grandparent, brother, sister, uncle or aunt, whether of the full blood, or of the half-blood or by affinity'—that is to say, having the relationship through marriage. Where a child is illegitimate, the term 'relative' includes the father and any person who would be his relation as above if he had been the legitimate child of his father and mother.

There are rarely more than about a hundred mothers a year adopting alone, one reason for this being perhaps that women do not realise sufficiently often that this course is open to them.

---

[1] In England and Wales in each case.

I shall be returning to mothers adopting alone at the end of this chapter.

On the face of it, adoption by relatives might seem to offer a child the best chance of happiness. After all, the adopters are his own flesh and blood, and so might be expected to love him more than strangers would.

Perhaps, when the child is legitimate, things commonly do work out so in most cases. The adoption order becomes merely the legal sanction for a convenient and useful family arrangement.[1] But the situation may be different when an illegitimate child is adopted within his own family. One of the supposed blessings of adoption in the ordinary way is that it cuts off the present from the past and so gives the child an unshadowed future. But a family adoption does not do this. Too many people know all about the child's beginnings, and as we all know, family memories are long. The child starts off, therefore, with the kind of handicap that adoption by strangers could have removed from his life.

I know there must be thousands of families where a child adopted by his relatives is never made to feel any sense of stigma or strain. There are even cases where, say, the children do not know that their adoptive father and mother are in fact their uncle and aunt.

But I have also seen complications arising from family adoptions, so that I cannot be too enthusiastic.

But this should be said; family adoptions usually express true sympathy and compassion for the plight of a child whose need is there for all to see. The motive for adopting is therefore straight and simple, and arises primarily out of kindness. Where the cause of the child's problem is itself something simple, like bereavement, pity is sometimes enough to start the new relationship off on the right footing.

---

[1] But read Brenda Maddox's book, *The Half Parent*, if you are thinking of a step-parent adoption. See book list at end.

Custodianship

Under the Children Act 1975, in a section that may not come into force until 1977, there is an alternative to legal adoption for relatives (including step-parents) and foster-parents who are looking after children and want some form of security for the relationship. This is *Custody* (Custodianship). A custodianship order will give the new 'parents' parental rights and duties over the child, but these will not be as final, complete or far-reaching as in adoption. When relatives or foster-parents apply to a court to adopt a child, they may be told that they should apply instead for a custody order. In fact some step-parents have been told already (from 1 January 1976) that they must wait for the custodianship part of the Act to come into force, and not try for an adoption order.

But the whole idea is so new—custodianship being a half-way house between ordinary long-term fostering and legal adoption —that it needs much clarification by courts, lawyers and social workers. At this stage, the best preliminary is to discuss your wish to adopt with the clerk or registrar of your local juvenile or county court, and you will then get some guidance on how to proceed.

However, the following is broadly the new law that will be coming into force:

Applicants must have had the child living with them for at least three months before the application, in the case of relatives and step-parents, and twelve months for others (i.e. foster-parents), and the application must have the consent of parent(s) or guardians; *or* the child must have had his home with the applicant for at least three years if consent is not given.

Step-parents cannot apply for custodianship, under the new law, if the parent they have married divorced the child's other parent, and that parent is still alive and can be found. In such cases the divorce court may make a custodianship order, at its discretion. But those who have become step-parents following marriage to a child's parent who has not previously married or has been widowed or deserted may apply for custodianship in the same way as relatives and foster-parents.

Step-parents, relatives and foster-parents may still seek to adopt; but they have no *right* to adopt (nor has anyone else), and the new law means that their application to adopt may be barred.

One sort of case that influenced M.P.s, social workers and others when the new concept of custodianship was hammered out was that of Timothy, whose mother went away to join the W.R.A.F. and left him in her own mother's charge. This 'granny-mummy', who was in her early fifties, later legally adopted the little boy. She was devoted to him, but after a few years his mother, who was now legally his sister, came home to live and found a job locally. Unfortunately there was a good deal of bickering, and gossip among the neighbours did not help. The natural mother, becoming jealous of her mother's rights over the child, wanted to interfere in his upbringing. Although the little boy was supposed not to know anything about his tangled relationships, he probably did know, or if he did not, somebody would certainly enlighten him sooner or later. There always existed the real danger of mutual recriminations taking place between the two women in his actual presence.

Was this a happy adoption? It was not, and the risks in it for the child belonged to the situation as a whole. Given such a set-up, the feelings that were aroused seemed to be inevitable.

Good Motives Are Not Enough

The trouble is that although a baby may be transferred between relations in good faith, life does not stand still. The situation—which was an unsatisfactory one to begin with—develops in a certain direction, people change, neighbours interfere. If one decides to adopt a relative's baby, particularly the baby of an unmarried daughter or sister, one needs several qualities that are independent of a mere kind intention to do the right thing. One must be tolerant and compassionate, one needs to know one's own mind and mind one's own business. One needs a lot of common sense.

It is necessary to make a firm arrangement with the natural mother that she must keep out of the picture emotionally—which means even in custodianship—and preferably to live right away. If this is impossible, or the parties do not want to do anything so extreme, then there should be, for the child's sake, a family atmosphere that is easy going and kindly, with a great deal of love and laughter and still more common sense.

This may seem discouraging talk for adopters or custodians who take a sister's child into their home and bring him up as their own. I do not want to be too discouraging. There must be any number of happy family adoptions, but the adopters in these cases are sensible people with a sturdy, happy family background and the natural parent too has an understanding heart.

Unless it is quite certain that the mother will not interfere later on, as she may well be tempted to do, it is far better not to apply for an adoption order and so accept total *legal* responsibility for the child, for there are less drastic ways of helping one's own flesh and blood.

There are other situations where full adoption does not seem to be really satisfactory. For instance, sometimes a family adoption seems to be undertaken unnecessarily. I have seen several cases of adoption of legitimate children where no special purpose appears to have been served by the legal process. The child did not need the protection of the adopter's name, and would have been just as well off in every way if he had lived with them as an ordinary nephew. The meaningless complication of adoption in such cases is bad rather than good.

When The Mother and Her Husband Adopt

As the statistics show, a great many women adopt their own children born out of wedlock, usually jointly with the man they marry.

Here again, as with uncle and aunt adoptions, such arrangements may seem good and reasonable but have hidden snags.

One does not want to argue a mother out of adopting her own child jointly with her husband, remembering always that the court may direct the couple to become custodians rather than adopters, if it thinks this is more appropriate. If the husband is also the father, the marriage has the effect of legitimising the child, and adoption or custodianship is unnecessary. They do not have to apply for any order—it happens automatically.

But the possible psychological difficulties ought to be understood from the beginning, and the adopting couple should also understand themselves and their own limitations. That goes for either adoption or custodianship. One of the unhappiest adoptions I have seen resulted from a mother's inability to cope with the situation she had created by adopting her own illegitimate daughter.

One might suppose that the difficulties would come chiefly from the husband's side, as the sight of the child would be a constant reminder of things he would prefer to forget. But although this may happen, and be a matter of reproach, it is at least as likely that 'feelings' will start with the mother herself, for whom the child will be a perpetual reminder of guilt. Unconsciously, perhaps, this deep discomfort of mind may turn to resentment against the child.

One thing is sure. The child cannot be left in ignorance too long. He must be told about his adoption, just like every other adopted child—perhaps not so early, since so much else must be bound up with that first telling in his case. But knowledge must not be left to chance and to gossip. There will come a time, which will depend on the intelligence of the child and the sympathy between him and his parents, when somebody will have to explain the situation to him. At any rate the opportunity must not be delayed beyond the time when he would normally have access to his own birth certificate and require to handle it.

Perhaps the best person to tell in such circumstances is usually the adopting father rather than the boy's or girl's own mother. He can speak of his wife to her child with a sympathy and kindness she could not exercise on her own behalf.

One advantage of the alternative of custodianship seems to be that it makes it more difficult for the new 'parents' to maintain secrecy towards the child: for one thing they are not full parents, and the court that made the custodianship order can revoke it in England and Wales on the application of (1) the custodian, (2) the mother or father or guardian of the child, (3) any local authority in England or Wales. The idea is that the new legal relationship encourages honesty and straight speaking. Similarly in Scotland.

Mother Alone

Many people do not realise that a mother, acting alone and without a husband, may adopt her own child if she is aged over 21. (Neither she nor the natural father may apply for custodianship.)

From the end of 1976 a single mother adopting on her own, can no longer receive maintenance payments from the natural father. Also, the court will have to know the reason justifying her in excluding the natural father. (Adoption has that effect.)

Note that the law says an adoption '*may* be made'. All courts have discretion to grant or not to grant an order in any particular case, even where a child's own parents are the applicants. Thus any application may be refused on its merits.

Today there is far less need than before for this kind of adoption. New legislation has made the status of an illegitimate child comparable with that of one born in wedlock. Also, the social climate has changed for the 'unsupported mother'.

Yet, look at it as one will, illegitimacy is still a stigma on a child. Adoption helps to remove this. The mother is given the power to keep the facts from those who have no business to know them, if she wishes it.

Few Mothers Adopt

As we have seen, comparatively few unmarried mothers do avail themselves of their right to apply for an adoption order. Extremely few of them adopt their children as babies. This may partly be due to ignorance of the law, but more probably it is that any difficulties of illegitimacy do not begin to affect the child until he or she goes to school.

Perhaps mothers *should* wait for a few years before making a final decision to adopt legally. An unmarried mother must find out whether she is tough enough to endure the loneliness and the criticism, and loving enough to remain tender and compassionate towards the child however much she may blame herself. The boy or girl should never begin to feel that he is a burden, if not a source of shame. The best time to apply, therefore, may be when the child is between four and five—before school begins, and also before the child is old enough to be asked by the Guardian *ad litem* if he knows what adoption means and whether he wants to be adopted. Although of course older children should have their feelings consulted, it is far better that an adoption should happen before the child is emotionally implicated in it. It should take place above his head, in other words.

Any unmarried mother who needs advice and good counsel when considering whether to adopt her child—or have him adopted by others—might find it helpful to discuss her problems by getting in touch with the National Council for One-Parent Families, at 255 Kentish Town Road, London N.W.5, or she should find her local social services department helpful.

Legal Details

In general the requirements that govern adoption by strangers must be complied with when relatives or the mother herself apply for an order. Under the new Act, like other adopters, relatives, etc. must be over twenty-one years old—that means both, in the case of joint applicants; but at the time this was written the natural mother or father might still in theory be of any age, however young. Non-related adopters or one of them must be at least twenty-five years old until the new sections of the Act come in.

The mother adopting her own child, alone or with her husband, needs to undergo an investigation period, but not—under the 1975 Act—a fixed period, but just sufficient opportunity to see the child in the home environment. She makes application to the court in the usual way. As with other adopters, the child must be at least nineteen weeks old and at all times, during the thirteen weeks preceeding the adoption order, must have lived with her.

Payments made for a child under an affiliation order cease when the child is adopted.

But a word of warning here: a mother may, when she is living with, but is not married to, the father of the child, try to adopt jointly with him. She will find that she cannot do this, since only married couples may adopt jointly. She may then be tempted to allow the father to adopt alone, bearing in mind that perhaps he is able to provide financially for the child, and that the union appears to be permanent. Sometimes, too, adoption by the father enables him to claim increased benefit under a pension scheme, etc. Despite these inducements a mother should always think well before taking such a step because if an order is granted it means that she no longer has any legal claim whatsoever on the child.

There is also the quite different case of the widowed mother of a legitimate child or children remarrying and wishing to adopt jointly with her new spouse. She has the *legal* right to make application without even consulting the deceased husband's relatives, much less obtaining their permission; but she certainly has the *moral* duty of seeking their agreement. There are likely to be sentimental attachments, and if the child is a boy the continuation of a family may be involved. This kind of adoption, it seems to me, must often come under the heading of unnecessary adoption; but if people feel they must do it, they have no business to hurt the feelings of the other grandparents.

But here, again, as we have seen, courts in future, under the new Act, may require a couple to apply for custodianship rather than adoption in such circumstances. But at this stage I do not know the extent to which courts will prefer this alternative. There are objections as well as advantages in custody orders.

Summing up the whole position, under the new law, of relatives wanting to adopt, I do want to emphasise that the trend in future will be to discourage such adoptions (including those by mothers alone, which it is hoped to prevent entirely at some time in the future). The plan is that the child's security in his own home shall be achieved by means other than adoption.

14

Telling the Child

There is no more important thing in all adoption than knowing how and when and what to tell the adopted child, when disclosing to him that he was not born a member of the family

This is a well ventilated subject, since the correspondence columns of magazines and newspapers are full of it. Most people today would agree that a child must be told at some time, although there are still last-ditch supporters of the don't-tell brigade who would agree wholeheartedly with the lady who wrote the following to a newspaper:

'I don't care what you say, or what the psychological books say, I am certain it's wrong, wicked, to tell an adopted child that he is adopted. The truth ought to be kept from him at all costs. It would have broken my heart to be told I was an unwanted child.'

Many adopters who would not express themselves so strongly, nevertheless wish that their child need never know, and shrink from the whole business of telling.

Perhaps, therefore, since this is meant to be a book of facts and information, not a collection of theories about this and that, it will be best to begin by stating a few facts on the subject.

The first fact is that when a child is legally adopted, physical *tangible* evidence of his actual status exists *at all times*, in the shape of the copy of the entry in the adoption register, which becomes virtually his new birth certificate. The second fact is that this document must be produced at intervals throughout his life, in connection with schooling, jobs, life insurance, passports and so on. It is part of his legal personality. As an adult, the adopted person has the handling of this certificate, and will know its contents, even though the short form may mask the facts for a time. Despite a long-held opinion, none of the parties to an adoption have had a *permanent* right to secrecy.

Thus one cannot hope to be able to choose whether an adopted person shall know or not know that he is adopted. He must know some time. Some people have thought that the Registrar-General's records should be falsified to the extent of permitting a new birth certificate to be issued with the names of the adopters inserted as natural parents. But a birth certificate is a copy of something recorded, and records relate to matters of fact. A falsification of that kind would undermine the validity of all records. At one time, for kindly reasons, the practice began to grow up of permitting adopters to be recorded in parish registers as the natural parents when a child was baptized. For a time this was sanctioned by authority, until the Church of England realised that it brought into question the honesty of its official records, and stopped it.

In fact, the law has moved in the other direction, and the Children Act 1975 lays down that adopted people over eighteen have the right to information from their birth records. This brings England and Wales into line with Scotland. Adopted people will have to see a counsellor (in a social services department or adoption society) before getting the information, if they were adopted before 12 November 1975. This part of the Act will be in force at the end of 1976. (See p. 164.)

Adopted people under eighteen who are intending to marry can apply to the Registrar General for information from the records showing whether they and those they want to marry come within the prohibited degree of relationship for marriage. This is obviously useful. Natural brothers and sisters have, through ignorance, married each other in the past.

There still remains the important matter of when and how to tell a small child he is adopted.

A mass of evidence established by experience gained from so

many sources—studies of adopted family life, child guidance clinics, the juvenile courts, letters to the press—that few people now would deny its truth, is that the only safe time at which to introduce a child to the knowledge that he is adopted is when he is very young indeed. As we know more, the age drops still further, and today we believe that the best time for telling is when the child is too young to remember later any time when he did not know, and certainly too young ever to have been at the mercy of other children, or adults, who knew before he did.

Adolescence a Bad Time

Facts about one's life and one's physical origins have a most powerful emotional importance, for they are a part of oneself. That is the reason why adopted children who learn of their origin in adolescence sometimes react to the knowledge with considerable violence. A girl may run away from home and live on the streets, a boy turn to thieving or other crimes. Some adopted children have attempted suicide.

Probably the majority of those who learn too late do nothing wild, but their inner misery may last for many years, even for life. Judging from what adopted people have told me, in most cases the adoptive parents have no idea of the anguish they have caused.

The fact that adolescence is a bad time to tell is well known nowadays. If some adopters leave matters till then, it is probably because they are cowards about telling—not because it hurts the child to be told but because it hurts them to tell, and they cannot bring themselves to do it until the eleventh hour or after. Every year, the thing gets more difficult.

Adopting parents do not always understand that a child may be too old even at seven or eight, and I have known cases when even five was too old. It is important for the parent to get there first, otherwise an outsider will do the job for him. The more intelligent and sensitive the child is, the easier it is to cause him pain by leaving him in ignorance too long, and the earlier he should be told. The safest rule is to start telling almost before the child can talk, and long before he can understand what 'adopted' means. If we start trying to sort out the 'sensitive' from the 'tough' so as to work out a good time for telling, we may easily make a bad mistake, because this is never a thing we can be sure about; for instance, a mentally backward person may be very sensitive.

A child should be told before he can possibly understand what it is all about, because a child who is old enough to know what it means is already old enough to be hurt by the information.

It is not even as if parents can tell their adopted children at their leisure, just when they think they will. Time is against them. The new law underlines this.

Some Cases

This is the way a number of children learned of their adoptions.

Mark was six. He had just gone to school. One day he came home very upset and asked, 'Mum, am I your own boy? Richard told me I'm like Billy'—a neighbour's foster-child—'and you'll send me away one day because I belong to another lady.'

Shocked, she told him that of course he was her boy, but even then she did not tell him he was adopted at that time, as she felt he was still too young. For months afterwards Mark would wake up in the night, crying as if his heart would break, 'Don't let her take me away, don't let me go.'

Vera was five. When her mother had friends in to tea, she would play with her dolls' house in a corner of the sitting-room. Sometimes her mother would say confidentially to a guest, 'Of course she doesn't know she is adopted. But she's the dearest little thing. I could not love her more if she were my own.' For some time Vera made no sign that she had heard, much less understood, these scraps of conversation, but one evening, in the bath she suddenly demanded, 'Mummy, why aren't I your own? Why am I adopted?' Upset by the sudden question, but trying not to show it, the mother hugged the child and told her, 'What nonsense! But you *are* my own little girl. What on earth made you ask a question like that?' Vera asked no more questions, but merely stored up the problem for later elucidation. Later on she was enlightened by her friends as to what adoption meant, and a boy cousin confirmed the fact. When she was twelve, her mother, thinking it was time to tell, rather nervously broached the subject but Vera said airily, 'Oh, don't bother your head about all that rot! I've known it all for ages.'

Perhaps that mother was one of those who complain that their children never confide in them.

Charles was nine. There was a desk in one corner of the dining-room, the drawers of which were never locked. He was not a prying child, but one day when his parents were out and he was looking for a sheet of notepaper he came across some documents bearing his name. He read them, and put them back, saying nothing. For months he suffered agonies of loneliness and of feeling betrayed. He started bed-wetting and his work at school became very bad. Fortunately, he had a much-trusted aunt who visited the family at that time, and to her he told everything. She was able to talk to him quietly about his adoption, about how much his parents had wanted him, how dearly they loved him, how they had wanted to save him pain by not telling him he was adopted. In this way the situation was saved, but otherwise it might have become a case of permanent estrangement, because in their loneliness and bewilderment children cannot forgive.

For although as a rule children do seem to recover from the shock of finding out in the wrong way and at the wrong time, without becoming delinquent or psychiatrically disturbed, perhaps a more common danger with many children is that they will cease to trust their adopters—who after all have been living a lie with them even if they have never told a deliberate untruth —and may never believe in them again.

A child can, and often does, dissemble his knowledge for years, knowing all the time but not saying a word, even watching with a prematurely mature cynicism while his parents make fools of themselves. One grown-up adoptee told me, with unforgettable contempt in his voice as he recounted these things, 'They said what they liked. I let them get on with it, and they did everything they could to keep me from seeing my birth certificate.'

A child can learn in the wrong way through idle talk. A builder's labourer in a small village, working next door to the home of an adopted boy, saw the child playing in the garden and said to him without any particular malice, 'You're a bastard, sonny, you know that, don't you? The people you're living with aren't your own parents.'

If nobody else blurts out the story to the child, the adopters themselves may, in a manner they do not intend. Jennifer, aged ten, found out in the course of a quarrel in her presence between her adoptive parents. During it, the woman's inability to have children of her own was flung in her teeth as a grievance. The quarrel came to a sudden end when the parents saw Jennifer's stricken face. Both genuinely loved her—and each other—and they did their best to comfort her. But she cried for a week afterwards.

Adoption is never a safe secret to keep. It cannot be hidden for ever, and should never be hidden at all.

The Stages of Telling

So much for the negative aspects of telling. I put it first because it seems to me that the danger that some adopters will not tell at the right time is considerable, and for them the shock treatment is the only thing. Now, however, we can turn to the positive side and consider how to tell.

Telling is best thought of as a process that can be carried out in stages. It is not something that happens once for all, but like all knowledge must be learnt in a number of ways, over and over again, over a long period. From sex to scientific technology, we must gradually build up our understanding of a matter, and facts, as such, may be the least part of it.

Stay with the idea of adoption as a term of endearment. It is certain that small babies take in more sensations, know more, than one can easily realise. It is an emotional process rather than an intellectual one, but they know. To have the word adoption mentioned first and frequently, as a rhythm, as a sound, with loving and happy overtones, seems a good introduction. It is a good thing to establish right from the beginning that adoption is a happy thing.

An expert, who is also an adopting mother, puts the next stage in this way: 'The best thing is for the child to be told at such an early age that he feels that he has always known it. In any case he should feel he was especially chosen by his parents, and had another mother when he was born, as soon as he begins to wonder "where babies come from". Otherwise the adopters will find themselves in deep waters when they begin to explain the facts of life. The easiest way is to begin by telling the child stories about mothers and fathers who wanted a baby and never had one, and how in the end they heard about some babies who had no fathers and mothers, and chose one of them to come home with them and be their very own for ever and ever. The story can be varied in the telling—the characters need not always be human beings!'

Very soon, or a little later, the child will be told or will guess with great pleasure, that the story is really about him.

I like the story told by an expert of International Social Service, which reports the way a little half-Japanese adoptee with American adopters described how she was adopted:

'Well, once we only had one little boy, and so we asked the man if we could have a sweet little girl for our very own. He said we could keep her if we would love her and take care of her.'

Note the unconscious stress on the fact that the adopters were privileged in having such a treasure.

The idea of adoption develops in a child's mind in conjunction with some queer ideas and fantasies. This matters less when we appreciate that it is the way all knowledge comes to us, but good telling, so far as a small child is concerned, lies in giving him the essence of it in the form of a bedtime tale on the above lines, and in telling it often, with a readiness to elaborate or fill in details on request, as soon as a child asks questions. It is one of those stories that is usually demanded every night, and with repetition it becomes part of the folklore of childhood.

Everybody must make up their own story. But it is, really, always the same one. It can begin to be told when the child is two or two-and-a-half years old, depending on the degree of intelligence or interest.

Now when a child is very young he often asks questions without showing much apparent interest in the answers. But in his fashion he always takes in what he hears, and is sensitive to evasiveness or embarrassment. If mother does not want to discuss certain things, he will quickly grasp this, and will either push these subjects to the back of his mind, beyond apparent memory, or will remember them and ask somebody else. Either way, he will still get the feeling that something is wrong, and this will persist.

Telling adoptive mothers not to feel embarrassment is like telling somebody not to feel seasick, and it is probably useless to say, 'You don't need to mind telling, because the small child won't mind being told.'

But perhaps it will help a little to say instead, 'Whatever you feel and say, do it honestly and you will be all right, and so will the child.'

Once I discussed telling with a mother who told me that when her adopted daughter was seven or eight, the little girl—who knew she was adopted but had not learned anything more—came home and said that a girl at school had told her she had 'another mummy and no daddy'.

'I didn't know which way to look,' the mother told me. 'You

see, I'd been meaning to have a good talk with her for ages, but had no idea how to begin. I mean, it's very difficult, after all. So while I was thinking what to say, she burst out crying, and I burst out crying, and we had a cry together, and after that everything was all right.'

There are many different ways of telling—as many as there are adopters and children—but the essence of this particular telling was that while the child had realised with a shock that there was something unhappy in her background that she did not know, and that her mother had not wanted to talk about it, she also now understood that her mother shared her feelings of pain and that somehow they were both 'in it' together. More cleverness, less honesty, might have been unsuccessful.

15

More About Telling

Good telling must, I am sure, depend on a good general outlook on life, for if one is not honest and kind, how can one show either virtue in any particular contingency?

To illustrate this I will quote an excellent booklet about telling which is produced by one adoption society. 'The crux of the whole question lies,' it says, 'in the conception of parenthood, and the adopted parents must be quite clear in their own minds before starting to talk to the child. Parenthood consists of two parts. The first is the physical one of bearing and bringing to birth a living child. The adopting parents, having had no part in this, should never pretend that they have. If they do so, they are guilty of deception, however good the intention.

'The second and more important part of parenthood is the care and rearing of the young. Give duck eggs to the gentle hen, she will duly hatch them, although it will take her a week longer than she knows it ought to take, and she will faithfully rear her startling family ... St. Paul used the picture of the adopting father as a symbol of the Godhead. "We have received the spirit of adoption whereby we cry, 'Abba, Father'." This is the part undertaken by the adopting parents so we must never be in doubt about the reality of our parenthood. It is no sham or pretence but a very real thing and the state makes if a lawful thing.'

One's 'real' parents are in fact those who show it by word and deed. The society I have quoted, the Lancashire and Cheshire Child Adoption Council, showed how the concept of legalising adoption might be conveyed very simply. 'Of course, we had to send a message to the Queen to ask if we might keep you for our own for always, and she sent us a message to say, "Yes, you are the father and mother of this child, and your home is his/her home."'

For one must make quite sure that there can be no doubt in the child's mind about the permanence and security of the relationship. Later on, as likely as not, somebody at school, with fostering in mind, perhaps, will tell the child that he can be sent away at any time; or he will hear neighbours talking to the same effect. It is quite necessary to arm him early against assaults of this kind on his sense of security, as the unfortunate truth is that there is practically no end to the silliness of some friends and neighbours when dealing with adopted children. Nor are schools or the authorities always very wise. A friend of mine was interrogated about her boy's adoption by the school doctor, in the presence of her child, aged six, and that of the school principal, the school secretary and the nurse. Despite her protests, the offence was committed again at a later date.

Telling About the Natural Mother

Naturally the question of the natural mother must crop up sooner or later. How is she to be explained, what is to be said about her? Point one is that she should never be presented to the child in a bad light, or, even worse, shown as not having wanted him. Point two is that it is a mistake to say, 'Your mother was too poor, so she had to give you away', or 'She was ill and could not keep you'. The child may well come to think that if these things could happen to his first mother, they could also happen to his present one, and anxiety is the result. In adult life, some adopted people worry lest their natural parents are poor and ill and need help, and this has sometimes led to a prolonged search.

Perhaps most adopted people bear more or less resentment against their natural mothers because they feel they were rejected by them. This is a pain that is part of the adoptive situation, although it can be assuaged by the whole attitude of the adoptive parents. Recent newspaper stories about parents who give away their children are not very helpful to happy feelings about natural parents, however, because children read newspapers and in any case it is very difficult not to see headlines.

Yet behind many adoption stories is a mother who, far from giving her child away indifferently and callously, thinks of adoption as being the best way in which she can make amends and so give him the chance of a happy life with other parents. Such mothers do not forget the baby they bore. One mother wrote, years after the parting, 'The pain is everlasting.' There have been many such letters. We know that the mothers care.

In books, if a parent meets a child from whom she was parted when he was a baby, some natural instinct ties one to the other. Perhaps this link sometimes operates in real life, but of the adopted people I have known who have met their natural parents, not one has experienced any affection. On the contrary, if they do not feel complete indifference, they may confess to active dislike. This is an unhappy thought for mothers who have given up their children and is part of the price they pay, but it should help to reassure adopters, who have every reason, whatever they tell, perhaps the more they tell, to feel secure in the love of their children.

Some adopters prefer to say, quite simply, 'Your mother and father died, so you came to me.' There is good precedent for this, for it has often been put this way quite successfully, sometimes by people whose moral sense is to be respected, yet it seems to me to beg a large question. It is true that the natural parents have 'died', in a sense, to the child. Yet the adopters imply physical death, and this is the way the child understands it. As the child grows older and asks more questions, he may think that there must be a great mortality among natural parents of adopted children; or perhaps he wonders if he was told a lie. So we come back once more to the question of trust, what it means and how it is to be maintained through life; and all the time we come up against far larger problems of thought and conduct than mere adoption.

One thing leads naturally into another. Just as knowing he is adopted leads a child to ask sooner or later, 'Who *did* have me, then?' so, a little later still, will it be natural for him to ask, 'And who was my father?' Therefore the problem of telling about illegitimacy is part of the whole business of telling and must arise at some stage. Yet far too many people stop short in their task after mentioning to a child that he is adopted, without realising that this is not enough. Some adopters say, 'My child is not interested.' But probably this is an example of wishful thinking. Perhaps it may be true of a few who are either mentally backward, or who live intensely, and practically, in the present. But it is not true, I believe, of the majority. Ask yourself if your child is so unintelligent that he is incapable of feeling ordinary curiosity.

All the same, this part of telling is very difficult for adopters, and it would be really unhelpful to pretend otherwise. But it is far easier if the original 'telling' started off on the right foot. An adoptive mother told me, 'I informed Sarah that she was illegitimate, when she came to the age of sixteen. She didn't like it much, but she was able to accept it.' This, understatement as it undoubtedly was, puts the whole thing into a good perspective. It indicates that if telling has from the beginning been sensible and sympathetic, the completion of knowledge can be accepted and the life afterwards can be a happy and rich one, even if the child 'does not like it much'.

You may or may not agree with me that the above was an example of good 'telling'. I cannot think that such a fact can ever be accepted without some pain; but as it is a fact, and a vital one to a child's understanding of himself, it cannot be suppressed. Therefore, the wise adopter's task must be to help in its assimilation.

Some adopters realise this need very early in the adoption. One well-balanced and sympathetically interested couple, who had just taken a baby, said as they watched him crawling happily on the floor, 'It does not worry *us* at all that he was born out of wedlock. We think none the worse of him for that. But we wonder what he will feel like when he realises he is illegitimate?' The adoptive father felt keenly the way men at work used the word 'bastard' so lightly and so frequently. Would his son feel hurt every time he heard it? These sincere and articulate people expressed what many adopters must feel, although they—like other genuine and kind adopters—will certainly be able to manage well when the time comes. The main thing is to recognise the need.

When to tell about illegitimacy is another point. But no outsider can really advise about this, because of the differences of temperament and understanding of different children. Also it must depend on the whole situation. I have known a boy of eight to speculate on birth out of wedlock and what it might mean, and as this child had a good brain, perhaps it would be a good plan to tell such a child all he needed to know before the onset of adolescence and so without involving emotion. But many children would need to be adolescent before they could take in or seem to require the facts. The main thing is to be honest at every stage.

Need One Tell All?

But given that a child should be told so much, is one to tell him all? That is to say, should he be told the identity of his real parents and helped to find them if he so wishes? This, in practice, is a question that very rarely seems to arise in an acute form, oddly enough. When it does, it seems always to be associated with wrong or late telling. In such a case, the longing to know one's natural parents is an abnormal and sometimes a devouring thing, and the child seems always to be under some compulsion, and to be pursuing not his real parents but some idea that will heal his pain. As a psychiatrist experienced with adopted children put it, children want to meet the real parent later on because a fantasy parent dominates their minds. (This psychiatrist also said that the proportion of adopted children among his cases was not abnormally high.)

As I mentioned earlier in this chapter, adopted people have told me that when they have managed to find their mother they are disappointed, or perhaps actively dislike her, and this could well be because no woman could possibly match up to the imaginary picture they have painted of her. There is idealisation as well as resentment.

One can, I think, do a good deal to prevent the domination of a fantasy parent. Of course it is a common thing for a small child to imagine he has different, and much more important, parents than the ones he really has. One does not need to be adopted to get such ideas. When I had them as a child I thought the whole world was in a conspiracy of silence against me. At the same time, I knew perfectly well that it was all a daydream, and in time this faded away naturally. The adopted child may get such dreams too, in his case with more reason; for even when he has not been told, he has unconscious memories. But if he is honestly dealt with, his dreams will be harmless and die.

The paradoxical thing is that the more one tells a child, the less chance there is for ideas about natural parents to become morbid, which is possible only in an atmosphere of ignorance and evasion. There may be curiosity, but it can be kept well within reasonable bounds.

A postscript to this chapter, now that there is so much talk of 'permissiveness', and for the benefit of those who say, 'Nobody minds about illegitimacy any more': I am sure this is not true, and that illegitimately born people do mind. They mind being casually begotten, they mind being 'given away'. This is the heritage their natural parents have given them.

16

Final Words on Telling

What adopters really fear, throughout all their uncertainty about what to tell, is that at some stage the child will renounce them and state a desire to return to the original parent. Ordinary adopters, very conscious of their own shortcomings as human beings, wait for the 'moment of truth' when their children will suddenly wake up to the fact that their parents are not perfect. Or perhaps they imagine that a quarrel will send the adopted child spinning off in search of the other parent.

Yet, special cases notwithstanding, mere knowledge of origin does not produce such a wish, because, good or bad, adopters really *are* 'mother' and 'father', the people who through the years have established a special relationship that nothing and nobody can efface. Even if one hates a parent at some stage of one's life—which is common enough—that parent is still different in quality from everybody else in the world, because he or she is an intimate part of one's early feelings and sensations. In *King Solomon's Ring*, Konrad Lorentz relates the comical story of how he was followed everywhere by a brood of ducklings, simply because he happened to be the first object they saw when coming out of the egg and so became, for them, their mother. In a sense, all of us are ducklings in relations to the person who nurtured us. It is nurture that counts.

I am devoting a great deal of space to telling and everything connected with it because this is the central point about all adoption, the point where almost all the difficulty arises, and I therefore feel it will be helpful to try to anticipate and answer some of the queries and doubts that arise in adopters' minds.

Some of what I have written above came to me as a result of direct contact with adopters and adopted people, some was collected from what other people have written, or from the words of experts speaking to people doing adoption work. Much has come from talking to the people who arrange adoptions as part of their daily work.

One great expert on adoption, who has neither the time nor the inclination to write down what she knows (and some of the best of them are like that), once offered me the following thoughts when we were discussing telling, and I cannot do better than close this section with them.

'You must build up the child all through life to meet his own history.'

'Children take what their adopters feel.'

'You can say to them later, "Some people began with a raw deal, and you were one of them . . . it is just one of those things".'

'Adopters are showing all the time, in all sorts of ways, what they really think of the child's original situation, for instance by comments made in the hearing of the child when looking at a film or television play, where an illegitimate child or erring wife is shown on screen.'

'One has to tell the truth, but it is all very difficult if the truth is hard. For instance, if there is a history of incest or where there is some unhappy story . . .' The expert thought it was necessary to tell the truth, but not always the whole truth. 'I romance about fathers a bit—that is easier.' Easier—and more natural—because so very little is known in most cases about putative fathers.

'It is not a good thing to introduce children as "my adopted son/or daughter". Children hate feeling different. The thought oppresses them throughout childhood and it may help to create psychiatric disturbances in them and difficulties at adolescence.' A child who boasts to everybody about being adopted may seem more invulnerable, but really is not so. He should neither hide nor display the fact.

'Some adopters will not accept their own sterility. They sometimes reject the idea of telling, because they are ashamed of this.'

I could elaborate on this fact that some adopting mothers are
so deeply upset about their own sterility that they cannot bear
to tell the adopted child he is adopted, or if they tell, do it
imperfectly. However, the feeling of shame because one cannot
bear a child has deep biological reasons and so probably cannot
be helped to any extent by advice given in a book. But at least
it is possible to become aware of one's feelings and to get them
out into the light of day, and this will help you (if so afflicted)
not to make a weapon of them—either by showing resentment of
the natural mother, who was only too fruitful, or by pretending
desperately *even to yourself* that the child is the child of your
own body. But there does not seem much purpose in saying any
more on this subject here. Either you will know what I am
talking about and something will start working itself out into
the light of day, or else you will not, and I might as well be
talking to the deaf and blind.

A good deal of research and clinical discussion has of late
years taken place on the situation of the involuntarily childless. It
is now possible to give much help to sterile couples in enabling
them to have children—though the investigation itself can be
gruelling to a sensitive couple. In these days when it is almost
essential for applicants to have been investigated before acceptance by an adoption agency, there is less chance of people
remaining ignorant about their deeper feelings when they do
adopt. But some people show a special gift for fooling themselves.

Incidentally, it is all too easy to talk about what adopted
children feel. I do not know what they really feel, although some
adults have honoured me with their confidences about childhood
memories and later feelings.

Anyhow, adopted people do not feel *as a group*. Each one is
different, with different experiences. This may seem so obvious
that it is superfluous for me to say it; but the public at large still

expects adopted children to behave in certain ways. Friends, neighbours, relatives, let alone school authorities and psychologists, 'wait for it'. One can only hope that the more adopted children there are, the more they will be taken for granted.

I daresay that some years hence we shall accumulate more knowledge about what different adopted people feel about all the various points discussed in this and the previous two chapters, and will have to revise our ideas accordingly.

But I believe that all adopted people experience a distinct feeling of loneliness as they grow up. This is insufficiently understood by others; but adopted girls have told me that when their first babies were born it meant something special to them, to behold for the first time they could remember a creature of their own flesh and blood.

Scrapbooks

More than once in the past I have been impressed by the scrapbooks kept by some adoptive parents to illustrate the juvenile histories of their children. Done with inventiveness, not of fact but of presentation, and a little art of display, these records can be attractively vivid and useful, and the children love looking at them.

Such scrapbooks are certainly not used only by adopting families, for they grow out of the standard types of printed album which people often start but forget about after a month or two. One large family of mixed 'own' and adopted had a book for each child, which was his own private possession, jealously guarded in one case (not an adopted but an 'own' child), shown freely to the visitor by the other children.

But the scrapbook history has a special use for adopted children, because it is a means of building up their sense of personal identity. We ought to use every such means we can, as you will already have realised. Adopted children have a greater need than others because their first, perhaps unconscious, memories are sad and involved with a sense of loss: there is a deep instinctive wish to be reassured that they are loved and *demonstrably* wanted. Some of the happiest of adopted people, who assert that they have always felt secure and confident in their parents' love, have warned me that this ought to be stressed.

In these records, the emphasis ought always to be on happy things. If you yourself had a happy childhood, you have the relatively easy job of transmitting the happiness which was the natural atmosphere of your own family life; if, however, you had an unhappy childhood, you have the wonderful opportunity of turning your own home into something happier and more creative for your child, and so changing the family environment.

Our personal security and 'belonging', in which our deep roots grow, depend on our knowledge of what our parents were like, where we were born, what our ancestors did. The adopted child needs as much as we can give him on that pattern, and as there is often not much we can tell him about his natural beginnings, it is good to build on many of the other things that interest a small child.

Do not get a printed record book, with spaces for this and that, because it will not meet your needs. Buy a big note-book with a cheerful cover instead.

In this book, start his own record: date of birth, weight, colour of hair, place of birth (the real place, for children are always interested to know where they were born. Other children are sure to ask them, and how awful not to know!)

Insert details of the natural parents, such as mother's Christian name, age when child born, where *she* came from, details of her physical appearance—height, hair, eyes—her job, her tastes, her hobbies, so far as these are known; and any similar facts about the father that you happen to know. Then there is the date when the baby first came to you—which, incidentally, is well worth making into a special anniversary—and the circumstances of his coming—including whether he cried or smiled, and what everybody said about him. Put in whether you travelled by car or train, what the baby wore, and so on. There must be plenty of space given to photographs taken at various stages, including a pre-adoption picture, if you have one. A cutting of the newspaper announcement of the legal adoption, if any, or at any rate a note of the date of the adoption order, when the baby became legally all your own, is another must.

If, and when, the baby was baptized should also go in, and there are all the progressive details to be entered—weight, cutting of teeth, onset of infectious diseases; the first family party when grandparents and relations were invited to see the baby, and what they said; the first Christmas, and what the presents were; the child's first drawing and the first thing he wrote—anything and everything, in fact, that might be interesting to look back upon and talk about in later days, and that can be woven into the never-ending and never-too-often told story of how it all began, and which will show the joy and pride of his parents in having their adopted child.

A child adopted is not automatically, as some suppose, a happier and better person than he might have been if left in his original circumstances. There is merely the *opportunity* for him to begin again on a happier note. If he grows up in a truly happy home—which is more than just a 'good' or respectable or well-to-do home—where the happiness is inward, he has happiness as a life companion even if in later life he runs into difficulties or tragedies; the world then is much easier for him. Happiness can be passed on by inheritance through environment, which is just as real as inheritance through the physical genes, the most important factors for the small child being warmth, gaiety, courage and, of course, honesty.

17

Adopting the Older Child

In chapter 6, I said that, all things considered, it is best to adopt a very young child, a baby if possible. But it is not always possible, and also some people for one reason or another prefer an older child—or perhaps an older child is there already to claim one's interest and compassion. Today there is far more emphasis than formerly on placing older children for adoption. Books such as *Children Who Wait*, and other publicity, have alerted us all to the existence of thousands of older children in public care who need permanent substitute homes, and who can bring joy to their new parents. This may be achieved by adoption or by the new relationship of custodianship.

Perhaps it would be as well to put in a note of warning here. Some people want an older child because they think he will be easier to look after, particularly if the adopters themselves are older. If this is your own belief, get rid of it. Older children are not easier, in spite of the fact that they have finished with nappies, nappy rash and wind. They take more, not less, energy out of one; and apart from the fact that children are in any case rather wearing, a child adopted late, unlike the baby who can be moulded into family life and has no other conscious memories, remembers to a greater or lesser extent other times and other parents. Therefore, he probably has to go through a period of strenuous adaptation to his new home.

Then, too, such a child is by now a person who can literally stand on his own two feet. No longer completely helpless, he has a will of his own already formed. His early experiences may have made him distrustful of himself and others, full of fears, and perhaps withdrawn into some secret part of himself where he is difficult to get at. This last is particularly true of a child who has had years in institutions, cared for by a succession of people, none of whom stays long enough to belong to him.

In any case, older children (as well as babies) who may be available for adoption may have been born out of wedlock and usually have had a previous life that has fallen into one of two patterns: either they have stayed with mother as she has moved from job to job, sharing her uncertain existence in a succession of other people's houses, or else they have been in nurseries and children's homes, where they have been visited by mother occasionally or not at all. Either way, their lives have not been complete or satisfactory. This is one reason why some children are released for adoption at a relatively advanced age by mothers who have tried to keep them but find the task beyond their powers.

Again there are children who have been in care for a long time and whose parents have shown little or no sign of wanting them home and have neglected to visit them.

There is also, of course, the quite large group of children who have been boarded out successfully for years and whose foster-parents in many cases later want to adopt them.

When you decide to adopt an older child, all the arguments already put forward for going through the 'proper channels' apply with added force. Simply because the child is older he needs careful placing with specially chosen adopters. In practice, few adoption societies have in the past placed older children. The big children's organisations sometimes did so, having had homes and nurseries and a network of skilled and experienced officers. The practice among such organisations was to place older children first on a fostering basis, 'with a view to adoption later' if all went well, and this in principle is what still goes on. But these schemes have been extended to include a whole range of children at one time not thought to be easily adoptable, and the children—whether placed for instance by Barnardo's or a local authority—may be permanently fostered, with suitable safe-guards, or adopted according to their special needs and the legal position.

What matters most is what the children need most. Adoption is being used more and more parallel with fostering. All local authorities place children in foster homes who may perhaps be legally adopted by their foster parents later on. But do remember that most fostering is *not* done as a preliminary to adoption, and that just having a child in your care gives you no right to adopt, although as we have seen, under the new legislation, foster parents will be able to apply for a custodianship order after twelve months with the consent of the natural parents, and after three years without that consent. This gives a good deal of security because the child cannot be taken away unless the court cancels the custodianship order. (See p. 12. This part of the Act was not in force at the time when this edition went to press.)

Making Contact

One useful preliminary for those thinking about adopting an older child is to get in touch with a local children's home—there usually is one—and then take a genuine interest in all the children there, making friends with them by visiting regularly. Sometimes it is possible to become 'social aunts and uncles' to a child or children of a family, taking them out, having them for weekends, etc. which may satisfy your own needs! In any case, this is *not* with the idea of picking out a suitable child, which isn't on, but in the first place to see whether you enjoy having children around you and want to have a lot to do with them—and whether children like you. But don't make friends with an individual child unless you intend to keep it up. Dropping a child flat is very hurtful to him.

Perhaps the exercise will stop there. Maybe you give up, and that is a good thing too, in its way, as you find out quickly what doesn't suit you. Or you want to persevere with your idea of adopting a child. In either case you are now wiser than when you started out.

But would-be adopters of children with special needs, the children who wait, may find that in their area they have to persevere, have to be tough, to meet the children who need them. You may get the impression from television programmes that there are all those children waiting for new parents, and that is true, but your local authority may be one of those that say *they* have no children languishing in their Homes. That may be so, but they could help you to approach another authority that does have children. Get in touch with that very resourceful and persistent voluntary organisation, Parent-to-Parent Information on Adoption Services, and/or the Adoption Resource Exchange, whose addresses are at the end of this book. Both the P.P.I.A.S. and the A.R.E. are friendly and approachable, and can give you a lot of help and advice. You can join the first-named organisation.

But let us come back to your Home-visiting. You might possibly see there a particular child in whom you are interested and who seems to have no ties. If so, you must find out at an early stage if he can be adopted. Then is the time to get in touch with the authorities administering the home, because it is to them that you will have to apply and they will decide whether you can be foster-parents 'with a view to adoption'. (You must realise, however, that this approach may not be welcomed in every case by the senior officer who will have to make the decision.) Discussions with social workers will help you greatly in making up your mind. You must be prepared to learn that there may be good reasons why you will not be able to adopt a certain child.

As I have suggested, the most usual approach to adopting an older child—or fostering long term—is to visit the social services department in the first place, and discuss your hopes with the appropriate officer. You will certainly be fully vetted at that stage if they go along with your ideas.

If all goes well, the older child may perhaps come to you first for what is intended officially to be a short holiday—perhaps only for the day to begin with, and then for a longer period a little later. How long this cautious approach continues must depend on you, the child and the circumstances, as must all things in adoption. There is no absolute rule.

You may at first think you have taken a quiet, obedient child with not much spirit. In a few days or weeks you may change your mind and think you have a little devil on your hands—a child noisy, obstreperous and disobedient. The novelty of you having worn off, you are now going through your own probation.

Did you realise that you too would be on probation with the child? A child's unconscious motive in 'playing up' is often to make sure that you really do mean to keep him, really do love him even if he behaves badly, really are safe for him to love. This test will often be pushed to what may seem to you unreasonable limits, and you may be tried to the edge of endurance. This does not mean that you have no right to punish, but in punishing you must know what you are doing, what you are punishing. Above all, you will always have to show that you love and want him. A punishment that a child regards as just is in itself an assurance that he matters to you. Threats to send him back if he is not satisfactory, or expressions of regret that you took him, mean that it is you who have failed, not the child.

Sometimes a child who has been deprived of mother love begins with new parents by being over-demonstrative, and constantly demands extravagant signs of affection. On the other hand, sometimes a child will seem to have no normal springs of affection. Either way, he is gradually reassured and becomes more normal in his demands. The thing is, with such a child, that when love is first offered he is unable to take it.

In some cases the reserve may be broken up by a complete return to baby ways; the child goes through all the stages of emotional development until he reaches the stage normal to his real age. This may mean bed-wetting, extreme dependence on the mother, and so on—things that a mother takes philosophically when her infant really is a baby, but which are harder to bear when he is five or six.

Because these things happen, as a rule, according to a recognisable pattern of psychological crises and development (and we may develop through crisis), the skilled social worker can give real support to the new foster-mother when they occur. People who take on an older child without guidance, especially those previously inexperienced with children, are sometimes faced with things they did not bargain for, because they cannot sort out for themselves children's normal behaviour from the things they do under stress, and cannot adjust themselves to a new situation. It is very easy, if one is not careful, to begin to resent and take out one's disappointment on the child.

The Need for Patience

An expert on adoption, who is also an adopting mother twice over, has said some vivid things about how a child must feel when he is put down in a strange home.

'Those of us who were evacuated [during the war] know well the feeling of being suddenly uprooted and set down in someone else's house, and having to fit in with the ways of a total stranger. If adults feel this, what must be the reactions of a small child, whisked away from everyone he knows, and expected to conform to the ways of people he has never seen before? He is always puzzled, usually frightened, and often acutely resentful. He may show these feelings by whining, by digestive upsets, by "tantrums", or by thumb-sucking, nail-biting or bed-wetting.

'Adopters need to be warned, and at the same time reassured, about these possible reactions. They should spend a little time with him in some place he knows, before carrying him off; and they should enter into the child's feelings and not try to hurry him into accepting them as parents before he has had time to feel confident and secure with them. They need to be warned against trying to force him to conform with their ways, or insisting upon too many changes at once.'

You cannot say *you* have not been warned, and I hope you have been reassured.

There is a good deal of truth in the saying that 'anybody can adopt a baby and make a good job of it', if by 'anybody' one means ordinary kindly people of honest intent; but just 'anybody' cannot adopt an older child, successfully. No special brains are needed; some of the best adopters are ordinary homely folk. But in an especial degree, when the children are older, adopters need to have natural wisdom and be well balanced, and to have a generously warm feeling for children in general. This love of children-in-general is important, because however much one may love a youngster who comes into one's life beyond the baby stage, one is always a little more detached in loving—there is less of self in it. It is the tiny helpless baby who teaches his mother 'instinctive' all-absorbing, mother-love and this applies to both adoptive and natural mothers.

More compassion is needed, too, with the older one. For you are looking less for the attractive child than for the one who has not had a chance. This may not be your conscious idea, but it is probably at the back of your mind. Given understanding, you may then find yourself with the unexpected bonus of seeing the beautiful unfolding and revealing of a child who becomes the joy and solace of your life. The one who seems unlovable because he has never been loved, and uninteresting because nobody has ever taken a real interest in him, soon becomes cleverer, more alert, more beautiful than you could have dreamt possible.

But perhaps never without work, understanding, patience, and, it may be, secret tears.

It was a P.P.I.A.S. member who provided me with this story of an adopted child, which illustrates how tough and courageous the new breed of adopters has to be, but how rewarding is the achievement. It is reprinted from the professional journal, *Child*

Adoption (Association of British Adoption and Fostering Agencies):

We first met E. when she was seven, with her social worker in the park at the beginning of April. She had been in residential care all her life except for two unsuccessful fostering attempts. One or two other couples who visited the home were told quite plainly by her that if they thought she was going home with them to be 'their' little girl they had better 'go away' because she *wasn't*. After three very successful visits to us, one over-night, she came at the end of that same month to stay for good. Because of the previous failures and her particular character everyone felt it best if she were moved very quickly, once she (and we) thought this a good idea! She is basically a very happy, boisterous little girl but can put up her defences and become very aggressive as soon as she feels at a disadvantage. Our other children, all boys, had no difficulty with a 'sissy' girl.

From then on till Christmas we thought we were slowly progressing. We had problems, though, of course. There were attention-seeking show-off scenes, noisy, verbal aggressiveness and highly emotional bed-time scenes. These were deliberately provoked, usually by a very small naughty incident which was then blown up out of proportion by her to make sure we would give her lots of verbal and physical reassurance, and proof of our love. This was repeated nightly for many weeks, lasting anything from twenty to forty-five minutes, but as it became less intense we felt we could become a little firmer and not always allow it to happen, and slowly it disappeared.

Her efforts to divide the family, however, were more worrying. She had survived seven years of residential care reasonably unharmed because she was a tough, fighting extrovert. Somehow she had to come out on top, and of course this had to be at someone else's expense. She tried to continue this with us, but found that in a close, loving family, although everyone was ready to give her all kinds of support and love, no one would tolerate to be divided from each other. Although she had such tremendous spirit and such a sense of humour and fun, she did not want to please any of us, least of all my husband S. At the time when the adoption date was set things looked pretty precarious, but we thought that once it was all over and she really belonged to the family she would gain the confidence she presently lacked.

As soon as she discovered that a date was fixed she really threw the book at us. The bed-time scenes returned, she tried to shock S. in particular, with the dirtiest lavatorial words she had learned, used in lurid descriptions invariably at meal-times. She would beg him to put her to bed and as he bent down to kiss her she would violently pull his hair or nearly choke him by pulling on his tie. The final row came one night when she shouted at him, '. . . and anyway it's up to *me* to decide if I want to stay here, not you'. This was something we had not bargained for. By this time we were so distraught and emotionally drained that we felt we were cornered and totally unprepared to take on the responsibility of the adoption which was imminent. We felt we all needed a breathing space and so asked for a postponement of the hearing. We were lucky to have a marvellous social worker and talked to her at great length. In particular we found her most illuminating on behaviour patterns of deprived children. After some days of objective thinking we realised that we had become too involved in the child's external and superficial behaviour to view things in their true perspective. We discovered that in the irritations and hurtings in the petty things of everyday life we had lost sight of the original purpose of giving her the love and home she had always been denied, and that this deprivation had made her behave as she did.

We told E. it might be a long time before the judge could see us, as he was very busy. Immediately, the tension broke and our relationships became better than at any previous time.

She began to talk about her natural mother, very hesitantly at first, but with greater ease each time. It became apparent that she had built up the enormous fantasy that one day her 'real mummy' would come for her. This made us all realise that all the previous attempts at introductions had failed because she feared her mother would be unable to find her if she were no longer at the children's home. This also explained her reluctance to change her name. Once we had talked through all this and had promised her to help her find her mother if she still wanted to when she was older, she relaxed completely and spoke with pleasure and excitement about going to see the judge. For our part, with all the tension gone, we decided to apply for a new hearing date and she was adopted about six weeks later.

It is now three months since the adoption. Life goes on, some days good, some days bad, but they are never boring! We realise that however much you think you know in theory, it's never the same when it actually happens.

18

More about the Older Child
and Some Others

With a child beyond the baby stage there are a number of things to remember, not complicated in themselves, but having an importance that should not be underestimated.

When he already knows his own name, this should never be changed, except gradually and with his own consent. His name may be almost all he has of his own, to give continuity between the old and new life. Adopters always like to change names, but with the older child you should prefer to leave it alone except for some practical reason—for example, if another child in the family has the same name. If you want to change, tack on the new one and gradually drop the old. If the child is old enough, let him help to choose his name.

But what shall *he* call *you*? Even a quite small child may have had several 'dads' and 'mums' before he came to you. It is best to go slow, and be 'uncle' and 'auntie' at first. Often a child starts using the more intimate terms on his own account; sometimes he will ask if he can say 'Mummy' and 'Daddy'. Again, in the modern way he may call you by your first names!

Another of the child's few possessions is his birthday. Even the foundling child is given a legal birthday on adoption. A birthday is an important thing to a child, and indeed throughout life it never quite loses its significance. So it should be remembered with full honours; and adoptive relations should also be informed of the date, and if necessary reminded of it.

The third thing that many older adopted children up to the age of five will bring with them is the dearly-loved Thing, that treasure which they take to bed at night and reach for first thing on waking. It may be an old doll, or an ancient cot-quilt, but whatever it is, it is very dear and must not be taken away, and should be treated with respect. If it must be washed or repaired, then this should be done at dead of night and returned by morning. This is difficult with a quilt, but has been done!

Should the older child, say one over five years who remembers his natural parents, be encouraged to talk about them? Dr. Bowlby, who has done so much to popularise the idea that children suffer emotional damage if deprived when very young of a mother's care, wrote of foster-children that they are attached even to bad natural parents, and resent anybody else criticising them; so criticism is out. In fact, if a child shows any sign at all of wanting to talk about the other parents, it is good to encourage him in a sympathetic way. If it helps him, then of course talk to him about his old life. Some children will not want to do it, or will seem to forget quickly. But one can never be sure what or how much they forget, and it is now recognised that if a child is distressed or grieved, it is far better that he should show it and get over it more quickly. Ignoring a desire to talk will not make it easier for him to adapt to his new life.

This is partly because, as we now see, the 'quick, clean break' is not the good thing people used to think. The gradual parting, painful though it is, is the healthy way to get new ideas and feelings accepted. Do not be too upset by children's tears.

There are no absolute rules about the speed with which a child settles down, but the following is a rough guide. Between two and three years a child should be able to become a part of his new family without much difficulty, although sometimes an even younger child will take some time to adjust. One small child of eighteen months whom I knew was in his new home for six or nine months before beginning to unfreeze, although he was a perfectly good obedient child, clean in his ways, and intelligent. But he had been in a children's nursery all his life, and in coming out of this emotional deep-freeze, it took him time to warm up. The process could not be hurried.

One danger that threatens a child brought up institutionally is that he may be labelled mentally subnormal or educationally backward, and so unfit for adoption. Such children often seem dull because they have never been stimulated by the give and take of family life. Some successful adopters, describing their first impressions of the child of a year-and-a-half whom they took, said 'He was very pale, fingers in mouth, rather a dull expression, dressed dreadfully.' Not very promising, certainly.

In a nursery, there is an assistant nurse to every two or three children, a nursery teacher, plenty of food, plenty of toys. But such a group of very small children who have not yet reached the age when they are socially minded is a rather unhappy sight for the visitor, because all they do seems so aimless. It is mother who is lacking from the scene, and the children appear to be waiting for her. If a stranger enters, some child may run up eagerly and, as in one case, grasp her by the legs and say, 'Is you mine?'

I.Q.s are not absolutes, because their apparent rating has been found to vary with environment and at different times. An I.Q. can improve. Intelligence isn't a fixed quantity at birth which you can assess immediately. The capacity to learn and to improve with instruction, what we call intelligence in a school-child, can be increased if the environment is stimulating. This is true even of children rated as feeble-minded, as has been shown in a very important study done by the American pyschologist H. M. Skeels before the war.

But I am not referring here to the child supposed to be feeble-minded, but merely to one who seems dull and unattractive beyond the ordinary, despite the fact that there is nothing special in his heredity to suggest a low mentality. There is every reason to suppose that an ordinary affectionate home life will work wonders with such a child, although this does not mean that he will turn into Superman overnight.

The older child who lacks self-assurance gains a great deal from patient coaching in some special skill that gives him a slight feeling of superiority, in one direction at least. With a girl particularly, but for boys too, dancing, singing or elocution lessons are a great help, for physical control and cultivation of the body are important in the development of the mind. In many a cottage in a remote rural area I have seen a young executant quite ready to oblige on the piano, piano-accordion, violin or recorder, or to sing a little song as confidently as a robin. There is always somebody locally to teach these skills, and the adopted one benefits accordingly.

A little more should be said about the business of bed-wetting, for it has a considerable nuisance value, and is far more troublesome and widespread than many people realise. Some adopters seem to accept it, if it happens, more easily than others can, who get very worried. It may happen with any child, but especially with the insecure one; it has social difficulties and makes a lot of hard work for mother. Not unnaturally, adopters will hesitate before taking even an intelligent and attractive child who is an enuretic, or may think twice about keeping a child they are fostering who persistently wets his bed. But it is a pity to deny such a child his chance on this account, since insecurity and the feeling of not being wanted are so often at the root of the habit, and the condition will probably clear up when the child feels safe.

But it is no use pretending that this always happens. The cause may be deep, and the trouble take a long time to cure, particularly if the adoptive mother is over-anxious, over-protective or over-anything. Nor is the use of threats and punishments any good. Adopted people who lived for part of their childhood in old-fashioned children's homes have told me something about the punishments that were often employed, such as forcing the child to strip the bed and wash the soiled sheets, with everyone in the institution knowing of the crime.

Reams have been written about this subject, however, and, the best advice therefore is to obtain medical advice about a possible physical treatment for enuresis, and about child guidance clinics if the difficulty is psychological; also to have a stout and cheerful heart, as well as a stout and adequate macintosh sheet, or plastic mattress cover, to prevent the thing from becoming a tragic matter. This is one of the circumstances where a really skilled social worker 'on call' helps to give confidence. Incidentally, a child who never wets his bed may do so for a while when he is first set down in a new home.

There is a rule to be followed when a child is brought into a family where there are already others. Really this is no more than common sense, and it is strange that people do not always observe it. The child should not be of the same age or sex as the other child (if there is only one), and he should be younger, not older, than the child nearest him in age—the ideal is two or three years. I have seen some rather miserable adoptions where the adopted child is a kind of sandwich between older and younger 'own' children.

It is also highly desirable that the newly adopted child should not have been brought into the family to serve some purpose, such as that of being the companion of another child. There is a nice shading off of 'bad' motive into 'good' motive here, because it is regarded as quite permissible to want another child to complete a family. What in the jargon is called 'motivation' cannot be clarified by rule-of-thumb assessments, however, even though a host of textbooks have tried to instruct social workers on the subject. A good spotting point is to ask yourself if there is anything special—*anything* special—that you are expecting of a child you take into your family: to expect is to buy disappointment. There is the pseudo-beatitude which runs, 'Blessed is he that expecteth nothing; for he shall not be disappointed.'

One legal point to be remembered when adopting an older

child is that when your application is investigated for the court by the Guardian *ad litem*, he (or she) is bound to make sure that the child, if of an age to understand what is happening, knows that he is being adopted. The Guardian *ad litem* must be satisfied in such cases that the child 'wishes the order to be made'.

A More Helpful Law

Until the passing of the Children Act 1975, many children who might have been found a permanent substitute family, if not always through legal adoption, were blocked off from it; the law itself was an impediment to getting children out of statutory care and finding them new parents. The new Act should improve this situation for children actually in care, and it is intended to do so. Where parents have not been 'undertaking parental care', or have shown little interest in the child's welfare for at least three years, a local authority can assume parental rights and duties over that child. It can have the child fostered, and the foster-parents can later perhaps apply for custodianship. They will be protected in their physical possession of the child.

Foster-parents will also be able to apply for an adoption order in these circumstances, but the intention is that custodianship will be preferred to adoption by the court. The foster-parents can apply after the child has been with them for twelve months if the local authority, or perhaps a voluntary society which has placed the child, consents; or after three years in any case. All applications will be subject to the new spelled-out principle that the first consideration in adoption must be the long-term welfare of the child.

Apart from the law, however, we have found these days that it is not as difficult to find adopters for older children as we used to think. The public attitude is changing, and the professional case worker is learning new skills in placing children for adoption. There are often waiting lists for Asian, West Indian and other black children. We are learning more about what heredity is and is not. The crippled child, the one handicapped by the effects of polio, the spastic, the deformed, the child with a hare-lip or a strawberry mark, as also the child with a weak heart—all these may be happily placed in normal families.

From time to time I have met families whose adopted child has after adoption developed some physical trouble or disease that greatly handicaps him. The striking thing about these cases is the degree of love and loyalty that is evoked in the family; in them the reality of the adoptive tie, the truth of the relationship, is abundantly shown. Physically handicapped people, it is said, usually have cheerful and affectionate dispositions, and this is borne out by those that I have known.

Adoption agencies have till recently done comparatively little placing of children who are not physically normal in every way, and although the medical certificate that is required for every child who is to be adopted is not supposed to be 'a certificate of adoptability', it often works that way. Much more might be done in the way of placing children with a physical handicap, and indeed the agencies are gradually extending their policy to include such children. Children's organisations and local authorities, which are the repositories of all the children whom nobody else takes, have many such children in their care; they board them out when they can, and fostering may well end in an adoption. But a more active policy is being encouraged and, as I have said, new legislation is meant to help in this. But arranging such adoptions is very very expensive, *not* to the adopters but to the agency doing the placing. It may cost several hundred pounds. Up to a thousand pounds, in fact, an authority on the subject told me in 1976. But it can cost that much *a year* to keep a child in care, so it's a bargain if you like to look at it that way!

Although, of course, some non-white children are brought in from abroad in small numbers—e.g. Vietnamese or other Far Eastern orphans—most of the non-white babies are (1) born British, and (2) have one white parent. They have a difficult heritage in a Western world split into 'black' and 'white', but their sense of identity must include eventually an awareness that whether they like it or not they are the people in between. A child pushed into a black identity is not going to be any better off than the one brought up entirely to think and act white, when psychologically both have somehow to find a middle way. They could have a lot to give the world in better understanding, if only their adopters are well chosen.

I asked the adopting parents of a girl whose father was an American black, and who is now in her early teens, if they could give any hints for the use of others thinking of adopting a child with coloured blood. The little girl was placed at eight months, when the adopters were in their late forties. They have a definite religious background.

The adoptive mother, looking back, was sure that it was easier for them because they were an older couple. As she said, 'Usually older people are well known and established in life and in the neighbourhood, and are more able to withstand any adverse criticism or comment. Also, when one is older, one's family relationships are more securely adjusted. Having brought up a family, I did not find that general considerations of welfare troubled me, and I could devote more time to helping the child to adjust herself.'

This is the one kind of case where it does seem better for adopters to be older and, perhaps, to have grown up-families of 'own' children who are sympathetic to the newcomer. The grown-up children would always be very important, not only because of the child's emotional need to belong to the whole family but because, with older adopters, the question of long-term economic security is involved.

The fact that 'not everyone takes kindly to colour' does not worry these adopters, and the little girl has grown up with the children of her own age in her district and is accepted by them. The family only notice the feeling about colour when they go on holiday and leave the district where they are known.

Their adopted daughter knows there is a colour problem.

When she was a little girl she tried to scrub the colour off her hands and arms. (Another little girl came in from school one day and asked, 'Am I a darkie, Mummy? It's just my hair, isn't it?') She is an affectionate child, requiring a lot of understanding and sympathy, and is more easily upset and quicker to take offence than many children. She is a thoughtful and considerate daughter.

The adopters are aware that problems must arise, for although the is a good mixer and popular, and never lacks partners at social gatherings, she has begun to notice that her boy partners tend to invite other girls to visit their homes but not her. They think she may want to take up nursing. Obviously, adoption does not solve a black child's problems, and may produce a few for the adopters; what it can do is to give the background and stability of a happy home life, so that as an adult the child can meet what difficulties may come, well balanced and without bitterness.

Times are changing, and so are attitudes to colour. There are far more non-whites in the British population than ever before. They belong here and adoption can play its part in helping the far from easy process of integration.

Adopters have a real duty towards their non-white child in making good contacts with black people in their community, and understanding their way of life and ways of thinking. They should cultivate black friendships, and not try to make their child a white person in a black skin. They have to feel sympathetically what it is like to be black in a 'white man's country'. There are a number of publications now to help them. See the booklist at the end.

The Child with a Bad Parental History

Unless you specially choose it and were specially chosen, you would not consider, nor would you be offered, a child who is known to be mentally defective or one of those few who are so permanently handicapped by lack of love in early relationships that they are unable to form a loving relationship with foster-parents—these are the emotional cripples. But what about the child whose parents have some mental deficiency or abnormality. Just the statement that a parent is mentally defective, taken by itself, is 'an extremely unreliable piece of information', as an expert has said. The concept of mental defect is legal rather than medical, and the criterion social rather than intellectual. There are, too, many cases where a low-grade mentally defective mother has perfectly normal children. Also, many mental troubles are due to brain injury or disease which would not be inherited. An important point is that there are social factors that may cause a person to be labelled 'mentally defective'. For instance, a girl with small intelligence who gets into a moral difficulty may be labelled defective, whereas if she manages to keep out of trouble she gets on perfectly well in her own social surroundings without being regarded as subnormal.

Science is far less cocksure than popular opinion about the transmission of insanity or mental illness. Some mental disorders can be handed down, some cannot. There is a wide variety of mental trouble. If you ask whether mental trouble, as such, is serious, it is rather like asking if 'physical disease' is serious, when physical disease may be anything from scarlet fever or an inoperable cancer, which are not transmissible, to haemophilia, which is.

Today, when people pop in and out of institutions for the treatment of one mental disorder or another, and television programmes encourage more discussion and an enlightened attitude, we begin to get these things into a better perspective. A child with any kind of difficult background that may be thought to produce problems of heredity are in these days considered more readily adoptable than used to be the case. And not only the children of the mentally afflicted, but also children with incest in their background, the children of problem families or children who have had precocious and abnormal sexual experiences, among others. Many of these children are not suitable for adoption placing except with skill and care, and adopters need to be specially chosen too, because as has been said before, adoption is not a cure-all, or a form of treatment for anything. But in this chapter, which I think will be read only by thoughtful people, giving a permanent home to a child who lacks one, whether by adoption, fostering long-term or through custodianship, has its place, because for some it will be a challenge and perhaps the beginning of an opportunity.

19

Practical Points

The following notes mostly amplify or repeat in simple form, for ready reference, information given in other chapters of this book. Writing them has also given me the chance to say a few things it was not convenient to mention elsewhere.

Do not leap into adoption. You should think about it as carefully as you would think about marriage. There is the extra difficulty that you must make some kind of decision before you have even met the other party. You may find it helpful to discuss your ideas with a local adoption society or your social services department even if it does not arrange adoptions. Make it plain that you are just asking for information at this stage, not putting in a definite application. If there are local pre-adoption group meetings, do go. It will mean you can ask all the questions you want without feeling in the slightest degree committed.

When you feel that you are sure you want to take a child, consider carefully whether it is full adoption that you want, in view of all the circumstances, or whether you would like to foster a child on a permanent basis, with financial and other help from the local authority or children's organisation placing the child. Sometimes a foster-child may be adopted later, but *adoption and fostering are not the same thing*. Good foster-parents are always needed; adopters often have to wait for a child. As mentioned already, there is now this possibility of custodianship to safeguard a fostering arrangement.

Even if you experience difficulties and delays in finding a child when you apply through the regular adoption channels, think very carefully indeed before trying to find one unofficially through casual enquiry. Though soon private adoption will be prohibited you can still do it (1976), but the results could be unhappy. Read the earlier chapters of this book, not once but several times.

Do not advertise for a child or take a child who is advertised. If, for instance, you put an advertisement in a shop window, you may be heavily fined. If you take a child through an advertisement inserted by somebody else, or indeed take any child without full and expert investigation, you may land yourself in all sorts of trouble.

'Unofficial' channels include doctors and nursing-home matrons who arrange adoptions on their own. Such people may be very skilled at their own jobs without knowing anything at all about the requirements of good adoption.

If, without seeking it, you are offered a baby privately, get in touch with the social services department of your local authority and discuss the whole thing with them. They are not likely to help you to adopt the child, but they should be able to find out about its family situation and give skilled help if necessary.

If an adoption society or social services department decide not to place a child with you, do not take this as any criticism of you personally, or your home. Many perfectly good people have to be turned down for all sorts of reasons; there are so many people who want to adopt and, comparatively, so few children to be adopted.

The Probationary Period

If you are not adopting through an adoption agency, you must notify the local authority in your area that you have the child in your care and intend to adopt him. A simple form of notification is as follows:

To the Director of Social Services,
Blank County Council (or County Borough Council, etc.)

Re: (full name of child)
Born on (date of birth)

Dear Sir,

In accordance with legal requirements I/we hereby give notice of my/our intention to apply for an adoption order in respect of the above-named, who is my/our own child/step-child/foster-child.

Signature(s) of Applicant(s)

Do not forget to date this letter. Keep a copy of it, in a folder kept entirely for adoption business, and preferably not behind the kitchen clock. As mentioned earlier, your local authority may have its own form on which to make this legal notification.

If you, or one of you in the case of a married couple, is a step-parent, or relative of the child, *or* if the child was placed by an adoption agency or by an order of the High Court, an adoption order cannot be made until the child is at least nineteen weeks old, and has at all times during the preceding thirteen weeks had his home with the applicants or one of them. You can *apply* to the court before this, though, so that the case can go through as soon as this is legally possible.

Supposing you take a child aged three weeks, the first three weeks that he is in your care will not count, because the three months probation cannot legally start until the day he is six weeks old.

If you are not domiciled in this country (whether you are an alien or of British nationality) and are applying for a provisional adoption order, the probationary period is *six months*.

If you apply independently and not through an adoption agency (after third-party placings become illegal), and are not the parent, step-parent or foster-parent, then the child must be at least twelve months old and have been with you for at least twelve months. The local authority will be supervising you throughout. It will also supervise all cases of parents and step-parents adopting, and the adoption of children over the compulsory school age.

But I should remind you again—and this is a very confusing period in which to tell people about the legal aspects of adoption —that all this part of the Children Act 1975 referring to independent adoptions was not in force when this edition was published in October 1976.

Although the child must be continuously in the adopters' care during the whole of the probationary period, the court may take into consideration any period when he is in hospital or at a residential school, and grant an order if it sees fit. But the court, of course, must be told if the child stays away from home for any period or purpose.

If you want your identity kept secret from the child's relatives, you should apply for a serial number when making application to the court. Some, but not all, courts ask a fee for allotting a serial number. The county court charges a small fee for an adoption application; there is no fee in magistrates' courts, but in both kinds of court you are liable to pay any expenses assessed by the court. These are unlikely to be more than a few pounds. If you adopt a child through a local authority, the council may pay all costs. The cost of adopting in the High Court must include a solicitor's fee and will be quite expensive.

The registrar of the county court, or the clerk to the justices, as the case may be, will give you any other information you will need for completing forms and obtaining other documents, such as your marriage certificate (if you are adopting jointly), the child's birth certificate and the agreements of any parents or guardians. As a rule, adopters find court officials helpful.

In Scotland, procedure is similar, but the court is the sheriff court, in which legal representation is normally required. It costs more to adopt in Scotland than in England, as expenses almost always include legal representation. If you are willing for your means to be assessed, you may be able to get free legal aid.

Now, in both England (and Wales), and Scotland the adoption society may ask you to contribute towards the actual expenses of your case. Such expenses may be quite substantial but they will be related to your income. Societies still rely on donations, however.

Birth Certificates, Registration, etc.

A copy of an entry in the Adopted Children Register serves all the purposes of a child's birth certificate, and may be obtained from The Adopted Children's Register, Titchfield, Fareham, Hants. (telephone: 032-944 2511, extension 288). In Scotland, apply to Register House, Edinburgh. The shortened form of the certificate, which looks like the ordinary short birth certificate can be obtained for a few pence from the same source. But just because the short certificates resemble each other, do not think that this will enable you to conceal the facts from the child. The cost of the certificates in 1976 was 75p. and 25p. respectively.

Occasionally, under a misapprehension, some organisation— even a Government department—may demand the original birth certificate of an adopted person, or details contained on the adoption order. They have no right to do so, however, and the demand should be resisted. If you are in any difficulty on this score, write to the Association of British Adoption and Fostering Agencies, whose address is given at the end of the book.

Although for some years there was a practice in the Church of England of allowing, at the baptism of an adopted child, the names of the adopters to be entered in the parish register as though they were the natural parents, under the present Act the entry—and the baptismal certificate based on it—must describe the child as the adopted son or daughter of the adopters. It is desirable to wait until after legal adoption has taken place; otherwise the natural parents' name must be entered. If a child has been placed for adoption who has already been baptized he cannot be baptized again in his new name. But it is now possible to obtain a shortened form of baptismal certificate which mentions only the diocese and date of the baptism, and the child's new name. Ask your vicar about this.

If it cannot be ascertained whether the child was baptized or not, he may be given conditional baptism.

The Roman Catholic Church has a system of diocesan records of baptism and certificates can be issued in the new name without difficulty. With regard to other denominations, consult your own minister. (See also p. 95 for information about a 'Service of Blessing'.)

Nationality

An adopted person who applies for a passport offers his long or short adoption *certificate* (not adoption *order*) in lieu of a birth certificate, and officials are not entitled to ask for documents relating to identity at birth. He should apply not to a local office but to the Passport Office, Clive House, Petty France, London, S.W.1. But in the case of children adopted after 1 January 1950, when a new law came into force permitting foreign children to be adopted, evidence is required that the adopter (or the male adopter to a joint adoption) is a citizen of the United Kingdom and Colonies, as an alien adopted child becomes British only by virtue of the fact that he was adopted *in this country* by British people. (If they adopted him abroad, his nationality could perhaps be queried.) When an adopted person, who was not born British but was adopted by a British subject, fills in a passport form it is correct to cross out the printed alternatives, 'British by birth or naturalisation' and insert, 'British by adoption', giving the date of the adoption order. A child born here of foreign parents is British by birth. A British child remains British even if adopted by aliens who may take him to another country, unless he chooses when coming of age to change his nationality.

Although one country usually gives courtesy recognition to other countries' legal adoptions, e.g. in connection with passports and where the persons concerned are transients, there is still no general reciprocal recognition of adoption between countries. International recognition of the adoptive status has been achieved to a limited degree under the International Adoption Convention, signed by Britain and given effect here under the Adoption Act 1958 (but see p. 91). This is likely to be important chiefly in connection with wills and property. Therefore, if adopters (or adopted children when coming of age) have property or interests abroad, or the adopted relatives of children have such property or interests, they should always make a will clearly indicating by name those to whom they want to leave anything. This is one illustration of the fact that, although the Adoption Acts have tried to make the rights of adopted people as much like those of the natural children of a family as possible, no legislation is quite watertight.

So far as I know, New Zealand is the only country which at the present time recognises formally an adoption made in any other country, with the local exception of inter-recognition within the British Isles, and even here, Eire adoptions are excluded. New Zealand has a fine record of pioneering in adoption matters, and other countries have usually followed her example in the long run. Let us hope they will do so in this case.

Financial

Family allowances can be claimed in respect of an adopted child who is the second or subsequent dependent child in the family. They can also be claimed during the probationary period, but in this case adopters claim as the persons 'maintaining' the child, on a different form, 'Fam. 2', obtainable through any post office or local national insurance office. The natural mother should not be claiming the allowance at the same time.

Tax relief can also be claimed, not only in respect of a child already adopted, but for a dependent child before he is adopted, though not for a foster-child being maintained for payment.

Here again there must be an assurance that the natural parents are not claiming income tax relief for the child at the same time.

Under the will of the late Rev. W. F. Buttle, a trust fund operates in this country to help adopted children whose adopters can no longer care for them, the secondary purposes of the Trust being to assist unmarried mothers to bring up their children, and to carry out religious work in connection with adopted and illegitimate children. Letters intended for the consideration of the Trustees of the Buttle Trust should be sent to the Secretary, Audley House, 300 Vauxhall Bridge Road, London, S.W.1.

Adopted Persons: Access to Birth Records

If you are an adopted person over the age of 18 and want access to your original birth records, you should complete an application form obtainable from the General Register Office, Titchfield, Fareham, Hants, Box 7, PO15 5RU. (I am speaking of England and Wales. In Scotland, apply to the Registrar General in Edinburgh.) A condition of being given this information is that you should meet a counsellor, who will be an experienced social worker. The meeting may be arranged at the General Register Office, London; or the social services department of the local authority where you live; or the social services department of the local authority in whose area your adoption order was made. An appointment will be made for you as soon as possible but it may take a few weeks. If you live overseas, write directly to the Registrar General, who will advise you.

When you go to see the counsellor, you must take with you your means of identification—bank card, passport, driving licence, etc. The counsellor will have been given most of the information from your adoption order, including your original name, the name of your natural mother and possibly of your father too, and the court where the order was made. You can have any or all of this information. If you want a copy of your original birth record you can be sent one.

The counsellor may be able to obtain further information for you, but this depends on a number of things. Even if it was arranged by an agency the records may not be very full, and your adoption may have been arranged privately. The counsellor can give you an authorisation to obtain the name of the agency from the court record, if it is available. But adoption agencies in the past have only had to keep their records for 25 years and court records are not kept indefinitely. War damage, fire, changes of address, etc., may all make it difficult to get information.

You can choose whether you want access to your birth record or not, and whether you want just the bare facts or little or much additional information.

20

Scotland,
the Rest of the British Isles,
and Overseas Adopters

Although the British Isles are not very large, a number of different adoption laws operate in them. The distinction between the terms 'Great Britain' and 'British Isles' is therefore very important, although any citizen of any part of the British Isles, including the Republic of Ireland, is reckoned to be a British subject so far as the adoption law in Great Britain is concerned.

Apart from the adoption legislation which operates in Great Britain—England, Wales and, with certain modifications dealt with below, Scotland—there are different laws in Northern Ireland, the Republic of Ireland, the Isle of Man, Jersey and Guernsey. The Children Act 1975 applies only to Great Britain.

Although it is now unlawful to take a child abroad, out of Great Britain, unless he is your own child or ward or close relative, Northern Ireland, the Isle of Man and the Channel Islands are not reckoned 'abroad', although Eire is.

Below are brief details about adoption in the rest of the British Isles.

Scotland

Only some special points in which the working of the present Adoption Act differs in Scotland are given. Procedure is governed by rules laid down in Scotland, and not by the English rules, but the general effect is similar. The Guardian *ad litem* is there known as the Curator *ad litem*. An application is usually lodged in the sheriff court of the sheriffdom in which the adopters live, much less frequently in the Court of Session. Scottish juvenile courts also have jurisdiction in adoption cases, but few if any of them so act. In most cases the parties are not required to appear in court, and they are legally represented.

The child's consent to his adoption must be obtained if he is over fourteen years old (in the case of a girl, twelve). The rights and duties generally of the adoptive parents are the same as in England, but in Scotland these rights include the right to be maintained by their adopted child in case of need, because north of the Border the natural child has this duty.

There are special Scottish sections in the new Children Act 1975, but they have the same general force as the parallel English sections, and differences are fairly minor.

In Scotland the adopted child now inherits from the adoptive parent in intestacy, and a will merely mentioning 'my child' or 'my children' or 'issue', includes the adopted child. He may apply to the Registrar General in Edinburgh for information from his original birth certificate at the age of seventeen. He will be told that a counselling service is available either from a local authority or from the approved adoption society that placed him, if there was one. The situation is different in Scotland from that in England because adopted people there have always had 'the right to know' at age seventeen.

An adopted person in Scotland, as in England, who insists not only on knowing but in tracing his natural parents may find a lot that he does not like. It is true that there are people who feel they must know at any cost, but if the adopted person is inspired mainly by curiosity, then perhaps he ought to think again, and at least discuss it with his adoptive parents. No doubt, if he applies, the authorities will put this point of view to him. But his right to apply exists.

Scotland keeps its own Adopted Children Register in Edinburgh and returns separate statistics which show that about the same proportion of the population adopts in Scotland as in England and Wales.

Other Parts of the British Isles

In Northern Ireland adoption law is similar to that in Great Britain, and is based on it. A major difference is that whereas in Britain a minimum probationary period of thirteen weeks obtains, in Northern Ireland the same purpose is served by the granting of an interim order on first application, which gives custody of the child to the applicant for 'not less than three months and not more than two years'. This serves as a probationary period and the local authority makes all the necessary investigations during that time. A difference of vast importance to the adopters is that, unlike the position in England and Wales, children may not be placed for adoption without the prior written consent of the local authority. Rights of inheritance are similar to those in England and Wales, that is, the child inherits from the adoptive and not from the natural family.[1]

Costs of adopting in Northern Ireland include stamp charges and a solicitor's fee, legal representation being normal. Adoption is through the Supreme Court or the county court. Northern Ireland permits children to be taken outside its jurisdiction only by relatives or by people of British nationality who have obtained the necessary licence from a court.

Adoption law in the Republic of Ireland is different from that elsewhere in the British Isles, and reflects the Roman Catholic faith of the country and its views on family life and illegitimacy. Adoption orders are granted, not in the ordinary courts, but by

[1] Since the passing of the Children Act 1975, which does not cover Northern Ireland, the differences have widened. In 1976 it remained to be seen if and how comparable changes in Northern Ireland adoption would be made, and when. Adopted children there, for instance, still had no hope of a legal right to information about their natural parents.

a specially constituted Adoption Board. Adopters must be Irish and resident in the country for at least a year before the making of the adoption order, although aliens who have resided for over five years can also adopt. Legitimate children may not be adopted unless they are full orphans. The illegitimate children of married women also cannot be adopted, although a child may stay adopted even though his natural parents marry each other after his adoption, provided both parents gave their consent.[1] Illegitimate children of unmarried mothers may now, for adoption, be between the ages of six weeks and twenty-one years under the Adoption Act 1974. There is now for the first time a probationary period. Applicants must be married couples, or widows over thirty years old (couples who have been married over three years and who are both over twenty-five may also adopt), or the mother, natural father or relatives of the mother. The effects of the adoption order are more or less as in England, the child inheriting from the adopters. There are a number of adoption societies in the Republic and many children have been adopted there since the first adoption act was passed in 1952. Third party adoptions are now barred.

Adoption in the Isle of Man is almost the same as in Great Britain.[2]

In Jersey, under the law of 1962, which is based on English adoption law, the adopted child is treated in every way as the adopters' own child (including inheritance rights). This is true also in Guernsey, which gained its first adoption law in 1961. Procedure for legal adoption varies somewhat in the two islands, but in both cases the Royal Court in the island has jurisdiction, the hearings being *in camera*. In Jersey the children's officer makes all enquiries for the court; in Guernsey, where there is no

---

[1] A recent High Court judgment throws this into some doubt.

[2] At least it was until the passing of the Children Act 1975. But see the footnote on page 168 relating to Northern Ireland adoptions. There are now more local differences, and Manx adopters should consult their local authority or the court. This goes for the Channel Islands too.

children's officer, members of the Children's Board make the necessary enquiries, and the Board is the official body on that island which approves adopters. In Jersey the children's officer places most of the children, and there are very few third parties. There is an interchange of children for placing, both between the mainland and between Jersey and Guernsey.

When an adoption order is granted in either Jersey or Guernsey, the adoption is registered in the island. Births and adoptions in the Channel Islands are not registered in London.

An important point, for people who go to live in the Channel Islands and want to adopt a child there, is that both the Jersey and Guernsey courts are strict about proof of domicile. Applicants have to show beyond doubt that their residence is permanent. One employee of a mainland firm, to prove Jersey domicile, had to purchase a grave plot.

Non-Guernsey-born adoptees, though adopted by islanders, have not the right to buy properties at below a certain price. This may create practical difficulties for a Guernsey-adopted person in adult life, who is almost always a child born in Great Britain or elsewhere outside Guernsey.

In Alderney and Sark, which for most purposes are administered from Guernsey, there have not, I think, been any adoption cases so far. The Guernsey law does not mention these islands.

Adoption in Britain by Non-Resident British People

It is possible for people who are non-resident and/or non-domiciled to adopt a child in a British court under certain conditions. Perhaps for clarity the distinction between 'domiciled' and 'resident' should be made here again, as to many non-technically minded people the words may mean more or less the same thing.

'Non-resident' applies to somebody who does not live here but somewhere else. British people, for instance service personnel, who have a job which takes husband and wife for long periods outside Great Britain are non-resident in Great Britain, even though they may have property here and intend to return to the country at a later date. But they do retain British domicile, domicile being roughly equivalent to permanent residence where one permanently belongs. Domicile is something very hard to lose, and very hard to gain. An alien, who has not been naturalised British would be unlikely to obtain British domicile, even if he has lived here for forty years or more, the assumption being that one day he will return to his own country.

Non-resident British people may adopt fully in this country, provided they can fulfil all the other requirements of the adoption law.

Non-resident Britons must apply either to the High Court or the county court of the area where they are living for the time being (in Scotland the Court of Session or the sheriff court). They cannot adopt through a magistrates' court. Husband or, more usually, wife, must have been caring for the child in Great Britain for at least three months (thirteen weeks), but the other need only be here with husband/wife and child for long enough to enable the placing agency to have had sufficient opportunity to see the child in his new home. There is no fixed time limit under the Children Act 1975.

These provisions are designed especially to help people coming home to adopt, where the husband cannot stay for the whole time because of his job. But even so, the law's requirements do not make it too easy for the prospective adopters from overseas. They really mean that one at least of the marriage partners must be in this country for much more than three months in all, for the right child must first be found and taken into one's care before the probationary period can begin. This is no simple, speedy business, as the earlier chapters of this book show. It is desirable to get in touch with a suitable organisation before coming to Britain, so that certain preliminaries can be completed. A couple will not be accepted, however, until they have been personally interviewed in this country.

Provisional Adoption Orders: Adoption of Children Abroad

Under the Adoption Act 1958, the right was given to non-domiciled people (whether they were British citizens or aliens) to apply to a British court for a provisional adoption order in respect of any child (not necessarily British). The courts having jurisdiction are the High Court or county court in England and Wales, the Court of Session or the sheriff court in Scotland. The applicants must fulfil all that is required of applicants for a full adoption order, with the added precaution of a minimum probationary period of twenty-six instead of thirteen weeks, and the child must be at least thirty-two instead of nineteen weeks old at adoption. The effect of a provisional adoption order is similar to that of a full order so far as Great Britain is concerned, except that rights of inheritance and citizenship are not affected. The adopters must satisfy the court that they intend to adopt the child in the country in which they are domiciled, and full enquiries are made about them in that country to ensure that they are suitable persons in every way.

A British child adopted by an alien under a 'proposed foreign adoption' order does not lose his British nationality, and an alien child adopted in this country by an alien does not acquire British nationality. Foreign adopters should ascertain the position about nationality so far as their own country is concerned, and they would be very unwise to seek to adopt a child without first consulting their embassy or legation. The 'provisional' adoption order does not, and cannot, in itself give the child rights in any country but Britain. Some countries forbid their nationals to adopt or be adopted abroad, except with official permission.[1]

The main intention behind the granting of these orders, which enables American service people, for instance, to adopt while resident in this country, was as the Lord Chancellor said in the

[1] Under the Children Act 1975, there is a new section (24) covering 'Convention adoption orders', where child and/or adopters are nationals of the United Kingdom and/or a Convention country. Such countries will

House of Lords in 1958, to enable certain children to be adopted —for instance children with black American Army fathers. It also helps foreign and Commonwealth people to adopt their own children who were born here. Before the passing of the present Act, there was for instance, an English girl who had married an American and wanted with her new husband to adopt her child by a previous union; she found, however, that under the old law she was unable to do this. Now such a mother would be able to obtain a 'provisional' adoption order.

If you are successful in getting a 'provisional' adoption order, you can stay in Britain for as long as you like, in which case your parental rights are fully protected here, or you can take the child out of the country as soon as you please. In the latter case, the child's new status is not protected once he leaves these shores, so that it is very important to adopt him in your own country at the first possible opportunity. The evidence of the adoption order may be enough evidence in your own courts that the consent of the child's natural parents to his adoption has been obtained: this is important for in most, if not all, countries parental consent is normally required for an adoption.

In particular, however, there may be difficulties in connection with United States adoption procedure. New provisions were made in 1966 for the entry into the U.S.A. of, among others, non-American children under fourteen years of age going there for adoption. Adopters must, first, satisfy the U.S. immigration authorities (this is a Federal matter); secondly, they must obtain an adoption order in the State where they live, and most Ameri-

---

eventually be signatories to the International Adoption Convention. Many countries have been listed as agreeing to the Convention but very few have yet signed. You should consult a lawyer in connection with such adoptions, as indeed for any adoption involving non-British persons and/or property.

can adoption courts refuse to recognise a British provisional adoption order.

I cannot discuss the full implications of all this here, and

U.S. citizens who want to adopt in Britain should: (1) Adopt through an adoption agency which will help them with procedure, which is complicated and involves gathering a good deal of information; (2) Get in touch with the nearest U.S. Consul. International Social Service (Great Britain) should also be contacted when adoption is first being considered.

Do not be tempted to put off securing legal safeguards when you go home, under the mistaken idea (*a*) that there is plenty of time to think about that; or (*b*) that it does not matter anyhow. Not only will you have promised the British court that you will complete the adoption in your own country, but also your new parenthood will never be completely safe if you do not. All sorts of unexpected snags might develop, not least being inheritance rights, income-tax matters, insurance, even the death of husband or wife, and so on. We all live such complicated lives nowadays that we never know what may develop from leaving one knot untied.

USEFUL ADDRESSES

Association of British Adoption and Fostering Agencies, 4 Southampton Row, London, WCI 4AA (telephone: 01-242 8951)
The Association is the representative body of adoption and fostering agencies in Great Britain. It watches the interests of adopted people and adopters in regard to legal and official matters. It is not an adoption society, nor can it put would-be adopters in touch with people able to supply them with a child. It has a number of useful publications. See p. 177

International Social Service (G.B.), Cranmer House, 39 Brixton Road, London, SW9 6DD (telephone: 01-735 8941)
Has branches in many countries, and individuals as well as professional bodies can refer problems relating to inter-country adoptions to its social workers. I.S.S. does not act as a placing agency.

National Council for One-Parent Families, 255 Kentish Town Road, London, NW5 2LX (telephone: 01-485 8166)
The Council exists to give advice and help to one-parent families, a term which includes unmarried parents, widows, and others covered by the title.

The Adoption Resource Exchange, 40 Brunswick Square, London, WCI 1AZ (telephone: 01-837 0496/7)
Puts people wanting to adopt black children and others needing special care in placing in touch with agencies that could help them.

Parent-to-Parent Information on Adoption Services (P.P.I.A.S.)
A very active and helpful voluntary body, with many local groups. Hon. Secretary: Mrs. Hilary Chambers, 26 Belsize Grove, London, NW3 (telephone: 01-722 5328)

Children First

An excellent Irish organisation of those trying to improve adoption law in Eire. Secretary: Miss Ann Larkin, 16 Ballyroan Crescent, Dublin 14.

Telephone Advisory Services for those with questions and problems about adoption are now provided in Leeds and Cardiff by Dr. Barnardo's; and jointly by the C. of E. Children's Society and the National Children's Home in Woking, Surrey; East Grinstead, Sussex, and Bristol. Other services of the kind are likely to be provided in the future.

The Association for the Childless

A self-help group, started in 1975 by a sociologist, happily married but childless, who with his wife had found themselves subject to the stresses and strains experienced by so many couples in this very vulnerable group. Write to Mr. Peter Houghton, 318 Summer Lane, Birmingham 19, telephone 021-359 2113.

The National Foster Care Association

A very active and useful body, started not only to help foster parents to improve their own status and allowances, but to improve the quality of fostering and to promote better relationships with social workers. It has a large number of voluntary local groups. Development Officer, Arthur Burch, 129 Queen's Crescent, London NW5 4HE.

FOR FURTHER READING

BOOKLETS PUBLISHED BY THE ASSOCIATION OF
BRITISH ADOPTION AND FOSTERING AGENCIES
4 Southampton Row, London WCI 4AA

Adopting a Child. A brief guide for prospective adopters. Contains a complete list of adoption agencies, with notes on adoption law. There is a section on children with special needs who may be adopted through local authorities and children's organisations. 30p. including postage.

Explaining Adoption. A new guide for adoptive parents to help them in telling their children of all ages about adoption Illustrated with line drawings. 25p. including postage.

Adopting a Black Child. Family experiences of inter-racial adoption. Fifty-one families took part in a follow-up of their adoption of racially mixed or fully black babies when the children were from six to ten years old. 40p. including postage.

For Ever and Ever. Experiences of North American families who have adopted older children, adapted for British readers. 40p. including postage.

GENERAL LITERATURE

Yours by Choice. Jane Rowe. A book for adopters by the Director of the Association of British Adoption and Fostering Agencies. Routledge and Kegan Paul, 1968. Cloth, £2·00; paperback, 95p.

Children Who Wait. Lydia Lambert and Jane Rowe. Association of British Adoption and Fostering Agencies. £2·75 including postage and packing. Extracts of this book, for those who want a quick guide, available, price 25p. including postage, from A.B.A.F.A.

The Half Parent. Brenda Maddox. 'A compelling and immensely readable book' about step-parents and step-parenting which would be very useful to step-parents adopting, or to those couples seeking custodianship of the child of a previous marriage, or relation of one of them. André Deutsch, 1975.

Growing up Adopted. Seglow, Pringle and Wedge. National Foundation for Educational Research in England and Wales, 1972. A follow-up study of adopted children showing that the development of adopted children compares favourably with that of children growing up in one-parent families, and indeed with other children generally.

Adoption and Family Life. Margaret Kornitzer. Report of a study of 500 adopting families and adopted people. Putnam, 1968, £2·10.

Also

Afro Hair and Skin Care. Community Relations Commission, 15/16 Bedford Street, London, WC2E 9HX. Telephone: 01-836 3545. A valuable little guide for those who have black children in their care. Very basic. There are some food recipes too, for those with older children. Send large stamped addressed envelope.

CHILDREN'S BOOKS

Mr Fairweather and His Family. Margaret Kornitzer. The Bodley Head, £1·50.

The Hollywell Family. Margaret Kornitzer. The Bodley Head, £1·95.

Note: All prices are as at the time this edition went to press.

Index

Adopted Children Register, 93,
94, 161
  in Scotland, 93, 161
Adoption, assessment of suitability for, 22–26, 158
  beginning of legal, 16
  by aliens, 27, 92, 159, 162,
169, 172–173
  by foster parents, 11, 47, 70,
81, 137, 139
  by mother alone, 27, 90, 105,
109, 111–112, 113, 114
  by mother and husband 20,
27, 105, 109–110, 113
  by non-domiciled people, 27,
93, 159, 170–171, 172
  by non-resident British, 27,
91, 93, 170–171
  by private arrangement, 9, 12,
34–35, 46, 47–51, 58, 62, 64,
66, 70, 78, 81, 98, 158, 164
  by sole adopter, 27, 28, 37,
89, 105, 111, 113
  by step-parent, 13, 28, 36, 68,
76, 85, 106, 107, 159, 160
  consent and agreement of
parents to, 48, 69, 78, 82
  illegality of payment in connection with, 18, 46–47, 70, 77

international recognition of,
10, 91–92, 162–163
  irrevocability of, 23, 48, 87,
113
  jointly, 26, 27, 78, 105, 113,
160, 162
  law and, 26–28, 46, 55, 64,
75–86, 87, 112–113, 150–151,
159–160, 165, 166
  legal process of, 67, 70, 71,
75–86, 112–113
  literature on, 12, 30, 43, 55,
106, 136, 142–143, 177–178
  of children of divorced
parents, 36, 82
  of children of mixed race,
152–153, 173
  of handicapped children, 19,
29, 152, 154–156
  of own child, 19–20, 36, 68,
105–114, 160, 173
  pregnancy of adoptive
mother after, 73
  recognition of in U.K., 91,
165–169
  unnecessary, 13, 109, 110,
111, 113–114
  wills and, 10, 84, 90–92, 163,
167

179

Adoption Acts, 9, 10–13, 17, 19, 32, 34, 36, 46, 68, 69, 76, 79, 80, 81, 84, 87, 88, 90, 91, 94, 99, 105, 107, 108, 112, 113, 116, 151, 160, 161, 163, 165, 166, 167, 168, 170, 171

Adoption agencies, 9, 34, 44–46, 57, 64, 68, 73, 81, 85, 159
  advantages of getting a child through, 10, 44, 69, 75, 83, 97, 157, 158
  application to, 23, 44–46, 87
  attitude of, to non-religious and non-sectarian, 9
  denominational societies, 12, 32, 81
  objections of, 28, 32, 33, 36, 37, 39, 158
  unacceptability of atheists and agnostics to, 32
  visiting by officers of, 26, 68–69, 70, 99

Adoption certificate, 74, 92–94, 115, 162

Adoption order, application for, 26, 67–68, 75–86, 107, 113, 160, 172–174
  granting of, 15, 69, 74, 75–86 87, 92, 93, 95, 113
  legal effects of, 10, 87, 89–90, 92, 113, 162
  'proposed foreign adoption', 27, 159, 172, 173, 174

Adoption Resource Exchange, 139, 175

Advertising, illegality of, 46, 158

Age, of adopters, 20–21, 28–29, 35, 55, 113, 136, 153
  of child, 21, 52–58, 77, 80, 113, 134, 136, 150, 159–160, 172
  of child in relation to 'own' children, 57–58, 72, 101, 136, 150, 153
  of child, to be told of adoption, 84, 117, 120–121

Alderney, 165, 169

Aliens, adoption of, 27, 52, 92, 172, 173
  laws regarding adoption by, 27, 52, 92, 159, 162, 169, 172–174

Association for the Childless, 176

Association of British Adoption and Fostering Agencies, 12, 66, 95, 143, 161, 175, 177–178

Babies, adoption of very young, 8, 53, 137, 142
  as 'medicine', 23–25, 73
  learning to care for, 59–62
  medical opinion on, 65–66
  reaction of, to change, 54, 65

Baptism, etc., 71, 95, 116, 136, 161–162

Bed-wetting, 119, 141, 149–150

Birth certificate and record, 12, 74, 78, 88, 92–94, 103, 110, 116, 120, 160, 161, 164–165, 167

Birthdays, 38, 102, 146

Buttle Trust, 164

Channel Islands, adoption in, 166, 167–170

Child care workers, 47, 68–69

Children, adopting one or more, 21, 58
adoption of, legally adopted before, 87, 92
Asian, 8, 151
birth records, right to information on, 12, 93, 116, 164, 167
black, 8, 151, 152–154
'difficult', 48, 143–144
health and natural background, 64, 155
in care, 11, 18, 136, 139, 143, 151, 152
information illegally sought about, 94–95, 161, 162
mentally handicapped, 48, 118, 148, 154–155
'own' and adopted, 9, 33–34, 57–58, 72–73, 101, 153
physically handicapped, 8, 19 23, 29, 48, 152
supply of, for adoption, 11, 18–20, 41–42, 44, 139, 151
taking two or more at once, 58
telling facts of parentage to, 9, 64, 88, 89, 93–94, 110–111, 115–135
'unadoptable', 154–156
with bad parental history, 154–156
(*see* older children)

Children Act 1975, 9, 10–13, 17, 19, 32, 34, 36, 46, 68, 69, 76, 79, 80, 81, 84, 88, 90, 91, 94, 107, 108, 112, 113, 114, 116, 160, 166, 167, 168, 169, 171, 172

Children First, 176

Children's allowance, 71, 163

Children's homes, 19, 137, 138–139, 151

Church of England and baptism, 71, 95, 116, 161–162

Church of England Children's Society, 7, 22, 32

Clothes, 63

Consanguinity and adoption, 90, 92, 116

Consents and agreements to adoption, 49, 78, 79–80, 82, 83, 160, 167
to custodianship, 107, 138
father's, 48, 79–80, 82, 173
foreign countries requirements concerning, 173
mother's 55, 64, 69, 79, 173
mother's husband's, 79–80, 83
relatives of child, 113

Contraception, 8, 42–43, 73

Cost of adoption in England and Wales, 75, 85, 86, 99, 152, 160–161
in N. Ireland, 168
in Scotland, 76, 160–161

County court, 75, 76, 78, 84–85, 107, 160, 168, 171, 172

Court, application to, 26, 69, 75–82, 159
application to, for knowledge of 'natural parents', 93–94
hearing of, 11, 78, 79, 81–82, 83–86

Court—*contd.*
  informing, if child is away from home during probationary period, 160
  of Session (Scotland), 167, 171, 172
  refusal to grant order, 26, 36, 85, 108, 111
  revocation of custodianship by, 13, 111
Curator *ad litem*, 167
Custodian, application by, to revoke custodianship, 111
Custodianship, 11, 12–13, 28, 36, 76, 85, 107–108, 109, 111, 114, 136, 138, 151, 157
  by foster parents, 107, 108
  by mother and her husband, 110
  by relatives, 107, 108
  by step-parents, 107–108
  consent of guardians to, 107
  consent of parents to, 107
  revoked by court, 13, 111, 138
  unnecessary, 110

Departmental Committee's report, proposals of, 9
Divorce and adoption, 9, 13, 27, 28, 36, 82, 105
  and custodianship, 107
Dr Barnado's 22, 42, 137, 176
Domicile, precise legal significance of, 26–27, 159, 170–171

Eire, adoption involving, 91, 92 163, 166, 168–169, 176

Family, adopting a, 58
  importance of, to child, 9, 38, 100–103, 109, 133–135
  (*see also* relatives)
Family allowance, 71, 94, 163
Father, adoption by, 113
  agreement of, 48, 79–80, 82
  application by, to revoke custodianship, 111
  telling child of, 127, 136
  unmarried, and adoption by, 113
Foreign children and adopters, 52, 92, 162, 172, 173
Fostering a child, 22–23, 30, 47, 70, 76, 85, 107, 138, 139–140, 151, 152, 157
  payment for, 23, 70, 163
  with a view to adoption, 11, 81, 137, 139
Freeing a child for adoption, 10, 69, 81

General Register Office, 94, 164
Girls, preference for, 53–54
Gingerbread, 43
Grandparents, acceptance of adopted child by, 39, 100–102, 113–114
  adoption by, 19, 105, 108
  contact with natural, 64, 99
Group meetings, 45, 87, 157
Guardian *ad litem*, 79–80, 83, 84, 85, 86, 112, 151, 167
Guardian, application by, to revoke custodianship, 111
  consent to adoption, 107
  consent to custodianship, 107

Guardianship of Minors Act, 48, 82
Guernsey, 166, 169–170

Health of adopters, 32, 35
of children, 49, 152
Heredity, 19, 32, 48, 56–57, 155–156
High Court, 68, 75, 84–85, 159, 160, 169, 171, 172
Husband and wife, adoption of wife's child by, 20, 27, 105, 109–110, 113
joint adoption by, 27, 113

Illegitimacy and adoption, 13, 19–20, 42–43, 48, 56, 80, 84, 105, 106, 108, 109–112, 137, 164, 169
in Eire, 168–169
in Jewish law, 31
stigma of, 42, 106, 111, 129
telling child of, 110–111, 127–128
Illegitimate Children (Scotland) Act, 48
Income of adopters, 39
Income tax, 94, 173
Income tax relief, 71, 163–164
Infertility, 34, 45, 132, 176
Inheritance, and entailed estates and titles, 91–92
and natural family, 92, 94, 163
in Ireland, 90, 168, 169
in Scotland, 90, 167
not universally recognised internationally, 10, 91, 163, 174

rights in England and Wales, 16, 38, 84, 90–92, 102, 172
Institutions, danger of, 54, 137, 148–149
Insurance, 70–71, 94, 163, 174
Intelligence of child, 56, 148–149, 155
Interim order, 86, 168
International Adoption Convention, 9–10, 91, 163, 173
International Social Service, Great Britain, 174, 175
Ireland, adoption involving Northern, 92, 166, 167–168, 169

Jealousy, 33, 35, 58, 71
Jersey, 166, 169–170
Jews and adoption, 30–32
Jewish Court of Law (London Beth Din), 31
Juvenile court, 75, 76, 77, 83, 84–85, 107, 117, 167

Legal aid, 85, 161
Local authority, adoption placing by, 12, 18, 19, 26, 30, 32, 44, 81, 85, 137–138, 139, 158, 160
application by, to revoke custodianship, 111
assuming parental rights, 10, 151
children in care of, 11, 18, 19, 68, 139, 152, 158
informing of change of address, 70

Local authority—*contd.*
  notification to, of intention
  to adopt, 47, 67–68, 70, 81,
  158–159

Magistrates' court (domestic
  proceedings court), *see* Juvenile court
Man, Isle of, 166, 169
Marriage, adopted child's own,
  31, 92, 96
  certificate, of adopter, 160
  guidance counsellor, 25
  importance of stable, 37
Matrimonial Causes Act, 36
Medical certificate, 152
Medical opinion, importance of,
  32–33, 46, 65–66, 73, 150
Men, single, adoption by, 27, 37
Mentally handicapped children,
  48, 148, 154–156
Mixed families, 35
Mother, adopted person's wish
  to see, 88, 128, 167
  adopting alone, 27, 90, 105,
  109, 111–112, 113, 114
  adoption of own child by, 20,
  105, 106, 111–112, 113
  adoptive mother and, 49, 64,
  78, 89, 97–98, 108–109
  application by, to revoke
  custodianship, 111
  child reclaimed by, 10, 48, 69,
  72, 81
  freeing a child for adoption,
  10, 69, 81
  frequent disappointment on
  meeting, 64, 126, 129, 167

  in contact with adopters, 49,
  64, 97–98
  legal consent and agreement
  of, 55, 64, 69, 78, 79–82
  mentally defective, 48, 155
  not informed of adopters'
  identity, 64, 77, 78, 81, 88,
  97–98
  returning child to, 49, 62, 85
  telling child about his natural,
  63, 88, 111, 125–126, 134
  unmarried, 43, 80–81, 90, 108,
  111–112, 163
Mother and baby clinics, use of
  by adoptive mother, 60
Motives for adopting, 23–23,
  37, 108–109, 112
  for adopting older children,
  112, 136, 142, 150
  of mother for adopting her
  own child, 111–112
  wrong, 23–25, 37, 73, 150

Name, change of child's, 70–71,
  74, 78, 95, 96, 145, 146, 161–
  162
National Council for One-
  Parent Families, 43, 112, 175
National Foster Care Association, 22, 176
Nationality and adoption, 92,
  159, 162, 166, 172
New Zealand, adoption law in,
  91, 163
Non-resident British, adoption
  by, 27, 91, 93, 170–172
Nursery, adoption from, 52–53,
  54, 60, 63, 137, 149

Nursery—*contd.*
cost of keeping baby in, 18–19, 152

Older child, adoption of, 12, 19, 34, 54–55, 58, 74, 84, 136–156
consent of, for adoption, 151, 167
difficulties of adapting himself, 54, 136–145, 147–150
insecurity of, 136–137, 140–142, 149
making acquaintance with, prior to adoption, 138–141, 143–144
memories of natural parents, 136, 145, 147
staying 'on probation' with adopters, 139–140, 143–144

Parent-to-Parent Information on Adoption Services, 139, 175
Parenthood, assessing one's own ability for, 20–25, 45–46, 157
preparation for, 60, 63, 65–66
reality of an adopter's, 124–125, 131–133
Parish registers, 71, 95, 116, 161
Passport, application for, 93, 115, 162
Payment, illegal in connection with adoption, 18, 46–47, 70, 77
under affiliation order and adoption, 111, 113

Physically handicapped children 8, 19, 23, 29, 48, 152
Probationary period, age of child at start of, 55, 68–74, 77, 159, 172
claiming of income tax relief and child's allowance during 71, 163
for non-domiciled people, 159, 172
for non-resident British, 171
informing court when child is away from home during, 160
legal points, 67, 68, 70–72, 77, 159, 160, 167
official visitors during, 10, 26, 47, 68–69, 70, 160, 168
'Proposed foreign adoption' order, 27, 159, 172, 173, 174
Provisional adoption order, 27, 159, 172, 173, 174
Psychological difficulties, adoption as a cure for, 23–25, 37
of deprived children, 143–144
of older children, 103, 136–137, 140–144, 148–151

Relatives, adoption by, 19–20, 27, 28, 68, 76, 105–106, 108–113, 114, 159
custodianship by, 107–108
keeping child's origins from, 102–103, 160
of adopters, 38–39, 100–102
Related children, adoption of, 58

Religious belief, 9, 12, 31, 32, 36, 71, 81, 95, 161–162, 168
Research into origins permitted by Home Office, 96
Residence and domicile, 26–27, 159, 170–171
Roman Catholic Church, 30, 32, 168
and baptism, 71, 95, 162

Sark, 166, 170
School, telling child's origins to, 100, 103–104, 112, 125
Scotland, adoptions in, 12, 48, 68, 76, 88, 92, 93, 94, 116, 160–161, 164, 166–167, 171, 172
custodianship in, 111
Scrapbooks, 133–135
Serial number, application for, 77, 160
Sheriff court, 76, 160, 167, 171, 172
Single men, adoption by, 27, 37
Spinsters, adoption by, 27, 37

Telling child, friends and neighbours, 100–103
of adoption, 9, 88, 93–94, 110, 115–125

of illegitimacy, 110–111, 127–128
relatives, 100–102
school, 100, 103–104
Tenancy, protected, and adoption, 94
Third party adoptions, 9, 12, 34–35, 46–51, 58, 64, 66, 70, 78, 158, 169
courts and, 78
disadvantages of, 12, 35, 47–51, 62–63, 81, 83, 158
legal duty in, 47, 68
Twins and adoption, 58

'Unadoptable' children, 154–156

Visitors, official, during probationary period, 10, 26, 47, 68–69, 70, 160, 168
Voluntary societies, children in care of, 11, 12, 18–19, 69

Widows and widowers, adoption by, 27, 37
remarried and adoption of own child, 113
Will, making a new, 84, 90–91, 163
Women alone, adoption by, 27, 37, 105–106, 111–114

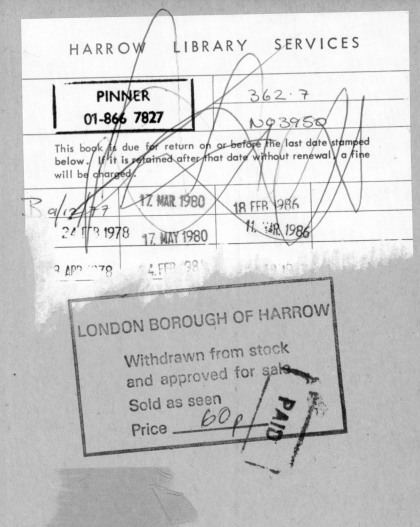